Patterns
of Promise

Patterns
of Promise

st. mary's college press ˢᵐᶜᵖ WINONA, MINNESOTA

Patterns of Promise
is edited and published by the Christian Brothers
with the following as principal contributors:

Louis M. Savary, SJ
George H. Kuykendall, Jr.
Brian McDermott, SJ
John A. McFarland
William H. Quiery, SJ
Philip Barry Osborne
Annette Cunningham
Ruth M. Cullen

Illustrator: Patricia Collins

NIHIL OBSTAT: William J. Tobin, STL, JCD, *Censor Deputatus*
IMPRIMATUR: † Terence J. Cooke, DD, *Archbishop of New York*
August 13, 1968

DISTRIBUTED BY
Holt, Rinehart and Winston, Inc.
383 Madison Avenue, New York, NY 10017
(Atlanta, Chicago, Dallas, San Francisco, Toronto, Montreal, London)

Printed in the United States of America
by North Central Publishing Company, St. Paul, Minnesota

Table of Contents

PART III:
THE STRUGGLE FOR UNDERSTANDING

Introduction

Introduction

Change in the World, Change in the Church

Today's world is being swallowed alive by change. More things have changed in the last generation than in the last dozen centuries. There is the electronic home, the computerized office, the mammoth shopping center. There are many new and exciting things to do. Some families now jet hundreds of miles for a weekend of relaxation. In the quiet comfort of home, there is a choice of continuous television entertainment — comedy, news, drama, sports.

Nor has change been limited to the material things of life. Catholics and Protestants now meet with one another and work together toward religious and social reform with new interest and enthusiasm — encouraged by the spirit of Pope John XXIII and Vatican Council II. In medicine, people apparently believe it will only be a matter of time before science can cure cancer, muscular dystrophy, and heart disease, and even prolong life by many years. In a few decades, space ships will carry commuters on scheduled runs to neighboring planets.

But progress is anything but onesided. Today the cities choke on automobile exhaust fumes, the smoke and smog of factories, the waste of urban society. The same knowledge which cures diseases produces napalm bombs, intercontinental missiles, and the terrors of psychological warfare. Students riot, ghettos burn, political leaders are assassinated.

Bus and subway signs remind people that they "can't get tomorrow's jobs with yesterday's skills." Workers find their training out of date after a few years on the job. The penalties placed on the uneducated are becoming heavier and heavier. It is an age of affluence in America but an age also of racial upset, mental hospitals, and dope addiction.

In the Church some feel that renewal is also out of hand, that the bomb throwers, clerical and lay, have all but taken over. There is confusion about matters of belief. Long-cherished religious traditions seem to be gone. Priests and sisters are leaving religious

3

life in great numbers. Some see change in the Church as full of promise, but many Catholics are angry, disappointed, and disillusioned about "renewal."

A Reaction to Change

There are various Christian reactions to change. One basic response is mirrored in a typical life situation.

A veteran teacher has held her own on the American high school scene for twenty-three years. Her teaching methods, growing out of hard work, were simple, practical, effective. Her rapid-fire questioning and daily deadlines produced generations of teenagers trained to the rigors of disciplined thought.

Sure of herself, sure of where she was going, she made her classroom a place where solid instruction prepared her students for survival in a difficult and sharply competitive world. She built a warm enclosure in which she nourished growing young minds and brought them to the frontier of adulthood.

For years the school board sent student teachers to observe her classroom techniques. Lately, however, new education Ph.D's from downtown have been visiting her office, bombarding her with notions about audio-visual aids, student-led classes, eight millimeter student-operated cameras. These experts are full of slick slogans about "fun" schools, "complementary" creativity, and "modular" something-or-other. Only when the experts fade down the corridor and out the front door, can she return to her classroom sanctuary, shut the door, and *teach* again.

Yet little by little the assault upon her professional life gathers momentum. Some few students, aware of the fun and games going on in other classrooms, start saying that her methods are old hat. She finds herself dropped without explanation from the city school system's curriculum committee. She is not invited, as she used to be, to draw up city-wide exams. In lunch-hour chitchat with younger teachers she feels increasingly outmoded, out-of-touch, lost.

What can she do? She loves her students and her school. She is too young to retire but too old to change. Is she only to watch helplessly while the progressives march toward what seems to her an ice-cream-on-a-stick vision of instant education? Maybe, she thinks, she's ahead of the times, while the progressives are nineteenth century Romantics, chasing after educational butterflies.

They are scrapping solid, proven programs for a mess of ill-conceived experimentation. She is terribly distressed. She has no way of coping with the new situation.

The World as a Nightmare

This teacher's problem may help us see the personal pain some Catholics are suffering because of change in the Church. All their lives they have had in their Catholic faith a fixed point of reference, a lighthouse, a kind of harbor or haven or refuge from the swirling confusion of today's world.

To them this world offers only distress. It gives them bad dreams. They look at the ads and the headlines, and they see a world of crashprone cars and air pollution. They see lots of con artists: corporate price-fixers, credit card economists, salesmen who are buddy-buddy till the thing breaks down and it's time to redeem the service guarantee, fast-buck promoters huckstering their "no-risk, high-dividend, fast growth" stocks.

For some it takes no more than the flick of a dial to turn the nightmare on: pious TV specials on sex and violence in society today are followed by TV commericals using women for the sexy selling approach, and by TV news programs picturing people killing other human beings in Asia, and zooming in on bloodshed in American city streets. They wonder about a nation where publishers vend obscene novels under the protection of the courts, where sensational papers and magazines sell millions of copies every day.

America may seem to them nothing but an acid-indigestion, tension-headache, worry-ridden society — an America of drug-takers, office parties, call girls, cut-throat interest rates, perfumed males, coddled minority groups, traffic jams, and sucker lists.

A Clearing in the Jungle

In the midst of bombardment from modern culture, a Catholic before Vatican II could (and often did) look to the Church as an oasis in the dry desert of this life, as a clearing in the jungle of the world around him. He used to be able to get off a hot, yellow bus and walk into his cool parish church, where, while sanctuary lamp and vigil lights flickered comfortingly, he could taste peace, listen for the voice of God, experience relief in a place where no storms came. There were no worries here about high price installment payments and taxes; war, auto accidents, riots, crime, and sudden death; hippies, sex, and smog.

There was more than the quiet comfort of the parish church for this harassed creature of God. In the Church's teaching he found sure guidance and sound doctrine. Here was a fixed signpost for a pilgrim lost in a valley of tears. Educated Catholics had their Thomas Aquinas or Maritain or the writings of Pope Pius XII. And in a world of illusions, in a crazy-colored neon existence, the ordinary person had timeless truth and his parish priest to point the way.

Sometimes it was a rugged faith, a tough voyage. There were crosses to carry. But the guiding beacon of doctrine was there to lead him to a good life and rest eternal. In a chaotic world, a soiled and messy world, the Church was clean, well-ordered, neat, and unspotted by the sins of mankind.

The Teaching of the Church

In the Church he found God — Father, Son, and Holy Ghost. God's grace — sanctifying as well as actual grace — was freely given. The Pope, vicar of Christ, represented God on earth and spoke God's will to man in infallible pronouncements, in encyclicals, and in special addresses. Catholic books, magazines, and newspapers spelled out the age-old faith in easy-to-understand language. Jesus, with Mary and Joseph and all the other saints, made intercession with God the Father for the Church on earth, for its members, and for the poor souls in purgatory. The rosary, novenas, stations of the cross, and benediction helped the people keep in regular contact with God.

Catholics had baptism to wash away original sin, confession to take away actual sin. God's will was expressed in the ten commandments and the six precepts of the Church. A hell of everlasting fire punished unrepentant sinners, while the good were rewarded with everlasting life with God in heaven.

Such teachings and customs provided the faithful Catholic with a clear-cut view of life. Protected by the armor of his faith, he could stand fast against the tide of materialism, secularism, and communism.

There were many things that commended the Catholic system to people of great intellect or worldly power. Numbered among Catholic saints were scientists and chancellors, artists and kings, wealthy women and philosophers. And in modern times, each year brought fresh news of important converts.

Change and the Innovators

Suddenly, almost without warning, in the late 1950's and early 1960's, the winds of change began to sweep through the Church. Familiar teachings — not only on moral matters like birth control but on fundamental principles of faith — were being challenged. Then came Vatican II, and in its wake came changes in practice and teaching that pained or alarmed or angered the traditional-minded Catholic. It was his Church that was being invaded, his way of life that was being threatened.

Today he sees innovators — some of them priests and a few of them bishops — loosening or questioning teachings on which he has built his whole life, his assurance of salvation.

Warned since childhood against "false Christs and false prophets," he now finds the modernizers rushing about upsetting things in the household of God. He sees these people as mindless revolutionaries, Mao-jacketed radicals, who call themselves Christians yet apparently feel that God is dead, who think of themselves as apostles of a gospel of peace yet seem bent on tearing down their Church and its time-honored practices.

Catholics Who Don't Care

The disturbed Catholic finds another cause of worry in certain of his fellow Catholics who are totally unconcerned about all the change. These people come out of the woodwork in this time of trouble and announce that they are unworried.

They do not love the Church. For them life has always been centered on self, family, friends, the nine-to-five job and the pleasures of the weekend. They were very little involved with the Church before Vatican II and are not about to get involved now. They go to Mass on Sundays, use the church for their baptisms, weddings, and funerals, sit silent in their pews while everything is caving in around them.

They seem to think that God — if there is a God — will reward their good works and Sunday observance. And if there is no God . . . well, for such people, "realism" means this: Year in and year out, the clock of human life ticks on, with no clear need for a Great

Clock-Winder up in the sky. People are born, live, love, die, and are replaced by other people. Each one, with whatever help he can get from the Church of his choice, has to find out how to live through his seventy or eighty years with a minimum of pain.

Change, Discouragement, Despair

Both the unreligious Catholic and the headstrong innovator cause irritation and anguish to the Catholic who does not want his Church to change. This irritation is understandable. The solid platform which sustained him in the confusion of the modern world has become a kind of skateboard, dizzily slipping and sliding in directions he cannot predict. He has nowhere to stand.

There are times when even a strong faith can be shaken. The changes, even though they come slowly and often almost unnoticeably at first, may seem to this kind of Catholic like the first tremors of an earthquake. He may fear that he was all wrong in relying on the teaching of the Church in the first place.

If he reminds himself of the doubts of St. Peter and St. Thomas and thinks of Christ forsaken on the cross, he may regain or reaffirm his faith. But voices, even voices from the pulpit, may again disturb him. And some few of these Catholics, facing the prospect of yet more change, are in fact so shaken that disillusionment turns to despair. And then some of them are tempted to abandon the Church completely.

Unshaken in Their Faith

Nevertheless, most Catholics troubled by change remain loyal to the Church. They are aware that changes in the world must in turn have their impact on the Church. But they feel that nothing other than externals of the Catholic Church will be affected — only, for example, such things as Friday abstinence or the use of English at Mass. Although the Church has become increasingly broadminded, the great central truths will stay as they are. What will remain, they feel, is the clear doctrine, the sound moral teaching, the strong educational system. Throughout all the storms of history, the Church has remained firm. It will continue to stand; for Christ himself promised that the gates of hell would not overcome it. Despite all the tumult and tension and chaos of modern life, the Church offers each faithful member a sure way to eternal salvation.

Catholics Who Want Change

There is another kind of Catholic who is not only undisturbed by change in the Church today, but he seeks it and wants it. He may agree that changes in the world are not always improvements. He knows all about unsafe cars, smog, con artists, drugs, status seekers, the cultural sex hangup, and all that. But because he is deeply concerned with truth and honesty in Christian life and with the larger social problems — war, poverty, hunger, disease, equal justice for minority groups — he sees a need for change in the Church.

He finds in the official Church a lack of concern for the individual. He sees the Church as a big corporation, and he may think that "renewal" of this corporation is all but impossible. He may or may not blame the individual priest or bishop for this. He usually blames "The Establishment" which locks them in. A favorite text for him is the word of Christ in Scripture: "Let the dead bury their dead. As for you: Follow me." He thinks that the Church concentrates too much on law (at the expense of freedom), and on sex (rather than love). He thinks that the official Church has a puritanical attitude toward sex.

He wants Christians to be pure, all right, but pure in the sense of being free of legalism and indifference. He wants to see the Church purged of the power-structure that makes it, in his view, a kind of totalitarian regime, like Naziism or Communism in its methods.

This kind of Catholic is trying hard, within his own circle of friends, to reach to the core of Christian life. He wants to be as thoroughly Christian as possible so that he can witness as a Christian in the contemporary world, and bring Christian love to bear on the world's problems. He does not look for easy solutions to problems in either Church or world. He is prepared for struggle and is willing to face temporary defeat. But he is impatient for change; he can be intolerant of people he thinks are standing in the way of change.

He is usually well educated. In many cases he can more than hold his own in theological discussions. He is aware of the many stages of development the Church has passed through in its history. This confirms his view that Christianity is no package, wrapped up, stamped "Made in Italy," and given to mankind, but that it is something unfinished, something still being developed.

A Church in Process

This Catholic does not believe that Jesus Christ founded a Church with frozen formulas to be accepted in blind obedience by everyone. The kingdom of God is not, in his view, to be enshrined forever in an institution supervised by an aristocratic group centered in Rome. The kingdom of God is the people of God. And he argues that this means that the people should elect their leaders on every level.

In any case, God's kingdom has not yet fully come but is in the process of coming and will be in process till the end of time. The Church is forever on its way to becoming a true people of God. It must be different in each age and always ready to respond to the needs of new generation. Change is the natural condition of the Church. Christianity has no choice but to grow with change — to develop, to evolve.

He is shocked by more conventional Catholics, whom he sees as anxious to turn the Church into a comfortable nest. "You can't go home again," he says. He finds in such Catholics a spirit of conformism that is as bad as the worst in modern American secular life — a no-risk, insurance-minded attitude that is anti-Christian.

He says that to look for security here is to evade the challenge of faith. To have faith means to plunge into the mystery, abandoning safety precautions and risking everything for the sake of encounter with the living God.

Radicals Who Want Revolution

This kind of Catholic may feel kinship with the great reformers. They too were usually considered heretics or people verging on heresy.

This kind of independent-mindedness, of course, can be a heady brew. Some radicals among this group talk almost as though they would not stop at anything. They do not want modifications, adaptations, reforms. They want revolution. Experiments in liturgy and parish life are to them very tame stuff. They are not at all interested in Roman approval of new usages. They want to turn everything in the life of the Church upside down. The Church's art treasures should be sold and the proceeds given to the poor. The Christian style of life must be thoroughly reexamined, reshaped, and remodeled. "Genuineness" and "relevance" are the only true tests. Everything is open to question — from the existence of God, to the moral law, to the doctrines of heaven and hell. Institutions should give way to free-form action groups. Priests, who should be celibate only if they want to be, should have no special status. Religious obedience is an outdated notion, they say, and religious orders are relics of a bygone era.

These radical people deeply upset the Catholic disturbed about change in the Church. What are these people going to do to his religion? The more conventional Catholic sees the Church in acute danger of being taken over by unshaven hippies, its Mass subverted by underground liturgies, its sound doctrine diluted by irresponsible and perhaps unbelieving theologians, its ancient precepts called in question by people who have no morals.

Questions about Change

If the traditionalist asks even the more moderate progressives for answers to certain questions, he is not likely to be consoled. For example, he may ask: What is all this change going to accomplish? The religious forms and traditions of the Church have proven themselves over centuries. Why is the faith that was good enough for our fathers and forefathers not good enough for us?

The progressive Catholic might answer: because it is for Christians of each age to find their own religious forms. We would be unfaithful to the Spirit if we merely relied on what was handed down to us from earlier times, even if it were perfect, which it is obviously not.

The questioner may persist: What assurance is there that change in the Church is going to be change for the better? What if the changes only lead to disintegration and loss of values, especially some of our most precious values?

That is the chance we'll have to take, the progressive might reply. To be open to the Spirit of God means to be open to whatever he will bring. God has given us no assurances that the future will be easy or safe.

How can such Catholics be reconciled? How can the Catholic whose reliance is on clear and unchanging Christian practices and formulas be reconciled to the other Catholic who is so concerned with Christian social commitment today that he is willing to see the Church of the centuries uprooted?

Today there are new theologies in the Church. Can any of them speak both to Catholics troubled by change and to socially concerned Catholics who want change in the Church?

Maybe a theology of Christian hope can. It all depends.

Tests for a New Theology

Any theology which will have meaning for both the "right" and the "left" in the Church today must meet many tests. Among them:

1) It must be based on belief in God, as understood by the Church throughout the centuries. It must remain aware that human concepts are little more than signposts, directional signals, pointers toward the transcendent God. Yet belief in God as revealed in Jesus Christ is absolutely essential. And this faith must be far more than a crutch, far more than the little white stick carried by the blind man — which only helps him find his way along a road he cannot see.

2) It must recognize and emphasize social problems — war, poverty, disease, race hatred, and all the other social ills which mock mankind. The old question, "What do I know?" has too often in its modern form become "What do I care?" We must care; that is the only salvation for our world.

3) It must be open to change, in both world and Church — and change even in matters considered by some to be unchangeable. Unless the Church becomes more flexible toward present realities and future possibilities, today's milestones of achievement may become tomorrow's tombstones.

4) It must be totally open to what is of value in science, history, sociology, art, and literature.

5) It must recognize the fact that there are many interpretations and religious views among Catholics today. There is great *pluralism* in the Catholic Church today — a fact not always acknowledged in the past, and a fact not noted in the general sketches of "left" and "right" given in this introduction.

For example, today's theology must face the fact that people who call themselves Catholics today split deeply on what they consider important. Deep differences in the content and quality of faith come from the fact that groups and individuals differ in their habits, experiences, temperament, age, sense of tradition, education and training, reading, and sense of loyalty; in their tastes, vision, and desire to conform or to challenge; in their wisdom, prudence, and many other aspects of life.

6) Finally this theology must somehow speak a single word of the Spirit of Christ to all these groups — *a word of reconciliation.* Christ's prayer was "that they (his followers) may be one" — as he was one with the Father. This oneness among his own was to be the sign to the world at large that the Father had sent him. There is no single mind in the Church other than the mind of the living God — a single Holy Spirit, but a Spirit who is heard differently by peoples of different personalities and background. Yet they are all one in the Spirit.

Part I
THE STORY OF THE FUTURE

Man
the Problem

chapter 1

A theology of hope is a theology that looks forward to the possibilities of the future. The Christian who hopes may feel profoundly the evil of today. Yet in Christ and in the promise of Christ's resurrection, he can see the world with a new kind of realism. Listening for what is really happening among men, listening also to the word of God, he struggles with the problems of today and probes the reality of today to find patterns of promise for tomorrow. His hope is for risen human life.

The Christian can hope because he lives in the light of promises made by God. The Christian can hope because he knows the history of God's faithfulness and his forgiving love. The Christian can hope because he knows God is intensely involved in the life of every human being, and in the life of mankind as well.

God is transforming and renewing the world. God is hard at work among men: building, creating, forgiving, purifying, inviting, challenging.

Man is the problem.

Human Suffering

In his play, *J.B.*, Archibald MacLeish has a word about "the problem of pain":

> "I heard upon his dry dung heap
> That man cry out who cannot sleep:
> If God is God He is not good.
> If God is good He is not God;
> Take the even, take the odd,
> I would not sleep here if I could
> Except for the little green leaves in the wood
> And the wind on the water."

Silence in the Face of Pain

Friends come to a person who suffers, knowing, at times, that their presence is all they have to offer. Silence is often one of the best of human responses. Even children recognize this. In the film version of James Agee's novel, *A Death in the Family*, young Rufus emerges from the wake for his father, and the other children surround him with silence. They are there. They stay close. They

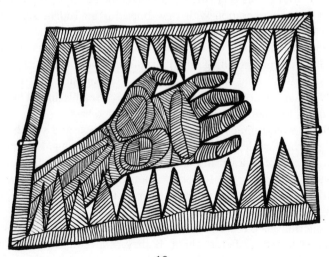

look at him. They may touch him. He knows that they know he
is now "special." But they ask no questions. They know that
Rufus is on another plane. He is suffering. And like most sufferers
he has no name for what he feels.

When theologian and scholar C. S. Lewis was plunged into grief
over the death of his wife, he wrote: "There is a sort of invisible
blanket between the world and me. I find it hard to take in what
anyone says. Or perhaps, hard to want to take it in. It is so unin-
teresting. Yet I want the others to be about me. I dread the moments
when the house is empty. If only they would talk to one another
and not to me."

C. S. Lewis wanted his friends simply to be present, but silent —
at least toward him. Suffering is a deeply personal experience. It is
too deep to be discussed, often too deep to be shared. One can only
experience it, never really cope with it.

People who suffer often feel that no one can say anything that
will make sense of the anguish or relieve it. Talk does little to
soften suffering.

Suffering often means "to lose what was hoped for." It happens
when the promise of human life has just not come true. Sleeping
children are burned and scarred for life in an apartment fire ignited
by a careless match. Like a dry leaf ground under foot, the promise
of their young lives is crushed in a few moments. Old people emerge
from a grave operation with new hope for an Indian summer in
their lives, only to spend these years as slaves to loneliness and
neglect. The fire of a young couple's love is snuffed out because of
a failure in understanding, cruelty, unfaithfulness, or betrayal. One
man steals all that another has saved. Sudden sickness or injury
puts a man out of work and abruptly reverses his life. There are
promises too many to count that do not come true.

Some would philosophize, as Aeschylus does, and say that suffering brings wisdom. Louis Evely adds that suffering also increases
our capacity for love and understanding. But it is important to
point out, as Father Evely does: "Undoubtedly, suffering sometimes
hardens us. It does not necessarily bring us closer to virtue. But it
always brings us closer to truth."

Suffering people see promises wither, watch helplessly as doors
of possibility close before them. If they believe in God, they often
turn to him. Some are angry with him. Some are mystified. Some

grit their teeth and try to accept the suffering. Some merely ask God, "Why?" Suffering is often a crossroads in a person's relationship with God. In his suffering, a person may say: "I will wait for God, for the present and the future belong to him." Or he may harden his heart and say: "God's promises are dead. I reject him." Every person's suffering may, therefore, bring him to a turning point. He may look hopefully toward God's future or rebel against it. If he opts in favor of the future, in favor of hope in God's saving power, the experience of suffering can help him mature as a human being. But it is not the suffering itself that brings the maturity. It is the deepened relationship to God and the renewed commitment to him *that does it.* St. Paul wrote: "We exult in tribulations, knowing that tribulation works endurance, and endurance works tried virtue, and tried virtue produces hope." Suffering is somehow the other side of hope.

Suffering and Job

Job is the classic Old Testament case of the man full of promise, like a young scientist might be today, or — and this is closer to the Job story — like a rich Western rancher with hundreds of acres of yellow grazing land and enormous herds of cattle. And then in a single day, Job was ruined. Land gone, cattle destroyed, family wiped out, all the promise of his wealth taken ruthlessly away, he found himself covered with ulcers "from the sole of his foot to the top of his head."

Three prosperous, self-satisfied "friends" come to talk to Job. They exude the old-fashioned wisdom. Job is a sinner. This is God's punishment. The solution is simple. Let him repent.

But Job knows he is innocent. And that's the lump of mystery that all his mental efforts cannot dissolve.

He rejects the quick answers of the pagans, as well: God is not evil, not a torturer, not a wild ungoverned power, not a natural enemy of man.

Worn down by the haranguing of his "friends," Job is reduced to silence and mute agony. And then the Lord appears. Not only the Lord's words, but his appearance, his presence, make a difference. When the Lord speaks, he does not defend himself point by point, or waste time on conventional wisdom.

"Have you an arm like God?" the Lord asks Job in a voice out of the whirlwind. "Where were you when I laid the foundations of the earth? Who enclosed the sea with doors? Have you walked in the hollows of the deep?" Job repents that he has questioned God. "I am but dust and ashes," says Job. "I cover my mouth with my hand."

Human wisdom and reason are ultimately helpless in the face of evil and suffering, says the Book of Job. Do not attempt to find justice in the world. Things will never add up and make sense. The innocent suffer. Thieves, traitors, and brutes prosper. Suffering is absurd and worse than meaningless — until a person begins to know God.

Yet knowing God and turning to him is no "solution" to pain. Job saw that. For the hurt and anguish, the senselessness, the unavoidability, the "why" still remain — locked in mystery.

The story of Job merely illuminates the option that faces a person in pain. The sufferer may allow his anguish to blot out all promise and hope. He may choose to build ever higher walls of isolation, of separation from others. To him, life becomes a miserable quarter-hour, with only a few very small, bearable moments.

Or he may put the hope of his life in the God who is creating the present and the future, the God who has not yet finished his work. And in this case, he often hopes "against hope" that such a God can be trusted.

Suffering and Christian Hope

There is then no "answer." The reality of suffering and pain is a hard, immutable fact of life that cannot be softened or overcome by talk.

But because faith and hope in the creative love of God are possible, a Christian can develop a lifetime perspective toward God and life that will enable him to hold his direction and confidence even in the midst of suffering.

All of us know something about the anguish of suffering. Though there are some who try to make light of another's misfortune and to cheer up the place with dishonest little speeches of solace, there are some who are quietly able to share the agony. They don't hand out sugar coated pills for instant relief. They don't try to say that pain is not pain. They don't pretend that they know how to suffer well themselves.

A man once wrote to a friend who was suffering terrible pain. The letter had only two lines: "I know it is unbearable for you. I wish there was something I could do."

A Christian may run into constant suffering and pain, and get knocked down repeatedly. He may try to get up and carry on as usual. He may get knocked down too hard, then turn bitter and lose his faith and hope in God. But even if he becomes angry with God or rejects him, he is still in a world which God is trying to transform.

God does not claim to enjoy the sight of suffering. He wants people to fight it, to work against it as much as they can. The world is filled with the ugly, disfiguring evils of hunger, poverty, disease, pain, war. To call this suffering blessings-in-disguise is dishonest. Jesus' response to it was to heal it, to stop it.

As suffering is to be conquered, so is death. Paul described it as "the last enemy." And the New Testament proclaimed Jesus as the one who heals suffering and destroys death.

God himself, in Jesus Christ, willingly entered this world of suffering. In fact he not only entered it but passed down into it, "even unto death." What makes suffering a mystery is not divine indifference to it but our inability to understand why it happens at all.

The picture seems to be this. God deals with man *as he is* — in a world where suffering and pain are inescapable. But God acts with, and within, the men and women in the world, healing and re-creating everything. His will is that man should be healthy, not sick; saved, not condemned; set free, not imprisoned.

Therefore, Christian hope rejects the idea that suffering is something good or desirable, and it points to Jesus Christ, who entered the world of man to heal suffering, conquer death, and give life. In Jesus Christ, God involved himself in man's brokenness that he might take him and make him whole.

The New Testament says that Christ told his followers to take up their crosses and follow him. Some Christians have twisted Christ's words to spell out a gospel of human evil as human good. They make it sound as though suffering were something Christ wanted and willed. Because of this suffering-is-good attitude, Marx could describe religion as the opiate of the people. Because of this attitude Swinburne could say: "Thou hast conquered, O pale Galilean; and the world has grown gray from thy breath."

But Christ's words about taking up the cross were not a benediction on suffering. They were a reminder by the writers of the Gospels that each Christian, trying to live in the Spirit of Christ, according to his faith and hope, will often encounter pain and suffering. Matthew says that when the Son of Man comes in glory "he will reward each one according to his *behavior*" — his actions, deeds, works. There is nothing wonderful about the crosses that have to be borne. They are the given, raw facts of life. God can make us whole despite the suffering that rips us to pieces. But that is no reason for praising suffering.

Discussion

1) Do you feel that this discussion really faces the problem of suffering intimately connected with Christian experience in ways that the book never mentions? For example, doesn't it make sense to think of suffering as a punishment from God? As a way of compensating for our sins? Or as a way of training us in endurance and patience? Aren't there many ways to reply to the claim that suffering is merely a necessary evil or an unavoidable consequence of human limitations?

2) As a Christian, how can you talk about God as all good, in light of the fact that the innocent seem to suffer with the guilty? Can Christian belief justify suffering that seems undeserved, or make sense of pain and anguish that seem meaningless? Is there any central Christian truth that can help a person maintain his faith in God in the midst of suffering?

3) The ancient Greek playwright Aeschylus said that the gods had decreed one basic law: man must suffer to be wise. Do you think this is a Christian notion of suffering? Recall what the Catholic priest, Louis Evely said: "Undoubtedly, suffering sometimes hardens us. It does not necessarily bring us closer to virtue. But it always brings us closer to truth." Aren't both these ideas of suffering really saying the same thing? What is your reaction to such statements? For example, how often has suffering in your life made you more open to the truth? Doesn't suffering have just the opposite effect, making people closed, bitter, and obstinate?

4) In your experience, does suffering bring people closer to God, or do they reject him as the cause of their miseries? Why do you think people react to suffering the way they do? For example, in

the story of Job, what difference does the Lord's appearance make in Job's attitude toward suffering? Why did the Lord's appearance have such a strong influence in Job's attitude?

5) Catholics sometimes speak of "offering up" their sufferings. What does this mean? Can one person's pain be helpful or beneficial to another? Do expressions like "offer up" have any meaning on the level of human experience, or do they refer to something supernatural? Explain.

6) If God does not enjoy the sight of pain and wants people to fight against human suffering, why doesn't he simply put a stop to it? Since he doesn't seem to be doing anything of the kind, what evidence do we have that the risen Christ has conquered pain and death?

7) If Christian hope, as this book presents it, seems to reject the idea that suffering is good in itself, is it good or profitable in any sense?

Sin

Everywhere We Look

The dehumanization of the individual is common in America. The job hunter often feels like a hunk of meat on an auction block. What am I bid? How much, how much? Feel that muscle, test that brain. He is a man for sale. He sits staring at blackboards scrawled with lists showing the going price for the services of those lucky enough to be chosen. He fills out fistfuls of forms. He answers questions. "Why did you leave your last job? Why do you want to work for us? What are you so nervous about? Here, fill out this form — and this one, and this and this. Don't call us. We'll call you."

The American man who has to immerse himself in some big, impersonal high-powered organization may find himself sliced off from his wife, his family, even himself. Almost no one ever really *plans* to ruin other people. But it can happen when he goes charging up that beautiful, beckoning ladder of success.

American cities and societies breed their own special forms of sin. Each social group has its own style of sin which newcomers quickly learn. Each group imposes conform-or-get-out rules on individuals. In some communities, religious bigotry and racial hatred are built right into the social structure, like a new car every year and the "right" summer camp for the kids.

Even commoner are the more subtle types of dehumanization. There are the daily pressures, complaints, and criticisms that grind down the contours of our ability.

There is the suspicion, anger, hurt, pride, the little bits of embarassing dust that collect in the corners of our everyday lives.

One common escape is the rationalization that *we* are the good people and that others exploit and injure us. Our army, our nation, our Church, our friends are the victims. The real trouble is with someone else, something else, some other group or nation or religion.

This black-white or dualist view is a little like a children's game of cops and robbers. There are good guys and bad guys. According to the rules, the bad guys are devils and breeders of evil, the good guys are saints. If the enemy has lapses of goodness and the good guys occasionally slip into evil, these are exceptions. According to the rules, the enemy can never change his stripes, and only total destruction will render him harmless. The game is: Name your favorite breeder of evil. Take your pick between Jews or Wasps, hippies or businessmen, loose morals or middle-class propriety, Karl Marx or Franklin Roosevelt, Ayn Rand or Stokely Carmichael.

Some people reject the idea of classifying the world into the good and the bad. They claim that there is no handy way to identify the bad guys and that there is no such thing as better or worse. They cannot see whitewashing one side, then blackening or destroying the other. They would rather interpret life in terms of style. The sole measure of significance for them is the way a person lives and dies. In the old films of Humphrey Bogart, for example, it rarely mattered whether the Bogey character was good or bad. It was the way the characters did things that mattered. It was his style.

Another popular way to duck the problem of moral evil is to deny it. Evil is here to stay, some say, so why brood over it? This attitude is common in the United States. Americans, full of that old pioneer can-do attitude, get annoyed when others dwell on mistakes and bad news. After all, they say, why cry over the past when there is still so much to do in the present and future. Some TV programs preach this gospel. Some *Readers' Digest* writers are on the stump for it every month.

But this gospel of sunshine holds no solutions. We are still stuck with the fact that men and societies sin repeatedly and deliberately. How can Christian hope respond?

Hope in the Face of Sin

Hope is a vein running through the whole of the Bible. "Where sin abounds," as Paul puts it, "grace abounds even more."

According to some theologians, the Old Testament as a whole tries to absolve God of the responsibility for evil. The Lord is good, and it is this that distinguishes him from the pagan gods. He is the creator, the rock, the savior, the Lord of goodness, creation and salvation.

How then does sin and evil intrude in the Lord's world, in the world governed by his saving power? It entered with man, with Adam. And from the beginning the Lord punishes man for sin with disorder in the universe, and, above all, death. But his heart is one of mercy; he promises a Messiah. This Messiah is the second and last Adam, Jesus Christ. Christ's central work is to overcome sin and conquer death; but his positive concern is for human beings, with whom he chose to share life. He speaks first and last of mercy for sinners, of salvation, of healing, and of hope both for this world and the next.

The biblical discussion of sin is brought more or less to a climax with the parable of the prodigal son. The son treats his father outrageously. But there is still hope; the son can change. He can return to the father against whom he has sinned — when he realizes the ruin his sin has brought. Most important, the father is not passively but eagerly waiting for the son's return. The message is not simply that in every chaotic stituation "there is *still* some hope." The message is that God is always a loving and forgiving God, and consequently every sinful situation is still *full* of hope.

Supported by Hope

What does the Christian say about sin? How does Christian hope respond when faced with the mystery of sin?

Though by his death and resurrection Christ guarantees that the power of sin is broken and will not ultimately triumph, sin's power must still be continually overcome in the people who are born into this world — by Christ's redemptive power working in them.

When we say that Christ destroyed sin's power, we mean that Christ made a difference in the entire picture, a difference of a completely new kind. It's a whole new world now. It is a world where Christian hope dwells. But sin is still in the world. Brutal men still break in, steal, and kill; children are still allowed to starve.

How does the Christian make sense out of this contradiction? How does he make sense out of the fact that some people turn to sin and rebel against God while others respond to God's desire that all men be redeemed?

Above all, the Christian affirms that God is love. But this does not add up to mere sunny humanism. God condemns sin; he does so repeatedly in the Scriptures. At the same time, God loves the sinner even to the point of allowing him the freedom to sin. God calls for a mature humanity, a humanity matured not only by human experience and human effort, but also by grace. But he does not turn against men and women for failing to be, as yet, fully human. God wants men to become more human; he does not want to destroy them. Thus the Christian must attempt to realize that we become less human — something less than what we are meant to be — when we turn away from what is right. We move against the tide of God's work in the world.

Both sin and grace are elements in a person's life from his first moment of existence. Each of us born in this earth enters into contact with a particular family, certain neighborhoods, a specific city, a nation. Nothing we meet will be perfect. To some extent, everything will be broken and twisted. We might say that a man inherits this situation of sin by being born into the human race. His life consists only of variations on it. This inherited twistedness is called original sin.

Original sin is explained in Scripture and in documents like Pope Paul's *Credo*, as the sin of the first man, Adam. Through Adam's disobedience, mankind was deprived of life; and the world was made subject to suffering and death. In experience, original sin is identical with the brokenness of the human situation, both as we find it in our family and culture and as we find it in ourselves. Every man finds himself somehow diverted or distracted from becoming fully human. He finds himself prone to selfishness and all kinds of human weakness. This is his condition from the day he is born.

Ordinary human sins (or "actual sins" as the catechisms have called them) are the conscious and deliberate actions or omissions a person makes that involve him personally in the original situation of sin.

There is, then, a distortion and a brokenness in the human situation and also in each man and woman (original sin). The human acts which break it up more are sinful acts (actual sin). Jesus made clear what sort of actions tend to injure, further distort, or destroy the human experience; and his two great commandments underline our greatest areas of responsibility: reverence and love for God, and real love for others. Ultimately, sins are all failures in love. Since it is love that humanizes the world, sin can be understood as any personal or group distortion of people. It is the personal rejection of God's will to recreate man. "Humanity" is "what God created men for."

Because original sin is part of every human experience, baptism becomes a new factor in a person's life. It is the sign of leaving one milieu and entering another, the experience of associating with Christians and their way of living. It is a clear affirmation of moving in a new direction toward true maturity, the full manhood of Christ. Baptism brings about a real change in our relationship to God. But if there is no genuine Christian environment or atmosphere, the

baptized person has little chance for growth in Christian awareness
and commitment.

Recent Scripture studies have greatly enriched the Christian understanding of sin. And advances in psychology now enable theologians to grasp better what sin means, humanly speaking. In the
past, it was often understood as the external way of measuring
our private relationship with God. In most catechisms some sins
were labeled "mortal," some "venial." A person who died with mortal sin on his soul, it was said, went to hell — even for only one
mortal sin. A person who died with venial sin on his soul went to
purgatory. When he had undergone the "temporal punishment" assigned to his venial sins — a punishment of fire very much like the
fire of hell — the person moved on to heaven.

As a result of this approach, many Christians closely identify the
entire question of sin, as well as suffering and evil, with reward
and punishment. People act, and God judges their actions; he either
rewards or punishes. Christian moral life — at least in everyday
practice — then begins to revolve around a simple code of do's and
don'ts. But it is hard to find room for the God of salvation in narrow
moral codes: the ten commandments, canon law, and so on.

God does not merely judge us; he saves us. He creates new
hearts and new ideas in men. Through people he is refashioning the
face of the world. Thus modern theologians stress God's concern
about world hunger, stockpiles of nuclear bombs, and the desperate
need of each man for work and dignity. God's concern, as conveyed
to us by Christ, is for *love*. Nothing angered Christ more than to
find religious people concentrating on "mint, anice, and cummin,
and neglecting the weightier things of the Law: right judgment,
mercy and faith." Do's and don'ts will never do more than serve as
a primer in morality; and in the long run, an itemized list of sins
may distract a person from the weightier things which simply cannot be classified.

Yet many people would still like to know which actions are sinful
and which are not. What response would contemporary theology
make to them?

What is really sinful and offensive to God and destructive of self
and society is any refusal to become more genuinely a person or
to help others to grow as persons. In fact, the thrust of the Christian
life lies in personal relationships among men and between men and

God. And it is impossible to list rules telling one person how to relate to another. Sin is too complicated to be explained by a handy, all-purpose code of laws.

There are pointers or guidelines like the ten commandments, the New Testament, the directives of the clergy and hierarchy, and the moral doctrine accepted in the whole Church. But often they fail to come to grips with the reality of sin itself. When we are guilty of listed sins, we may feel threatened with punishment like a disobedient child. But what we often do not realize is that we have failed in love. At another time we may fail to love as we should, without ever noticing that we stand condemned for our failure in God's sight.

Often, in fact, there is no "answer" — either simple or complicated — for the man who wants to do good and avoid sin. Only as God transforms human life do mature men appear. And only as men throw themselves into life, secure in the grace of God, can they hope to come to grips with sin.

Discussion

1) Many people would define sin as deliberately disobeying a divine command. Others would define sin as an act which makes a human being less human. Which definition would you prefer? Why? Which definition is more practical? Which makes the idea of sin clearer? Which corresponds more to your own personal experience of sin?

In the light of these two definitions of sin, discuss the fifth commandment. Are there more ways of killing a man than by murder? Can we kill a man's mind? Can we kill him by destroying his hopes? By depriving him of human dignity through economic, social, or political pressures?

2) Discuss some of the ways in which American society as a whole dehumanizes human beings: working people, children, old people, minority groups, people in depressed areas. Can these actions or failures to act be called sins? Whose sins are they? Does it make sense to say that our whole nation — or any other nation — is sinful?

3) Three types of response to evil are mentioned: the black/white approach, the stylist approach, and the optimist approach. Which of these approaches to sin and evil seems most common among the

people you know? Can you point out specific examples of ways that prominent leaders, newspapers, or television commentators use these three approaches to account for the existence of evil? Could any of these responses to evil be called Christian? Could they perhaps be part of a Christian response? Are there other ways of responding to the problem of sin and evil that are more realistic than any of these?

4) What does it mean to say that God forgives a person's sins, or that God's forgiveness makes a new man? Do you feel that in some sense sin and death have been conquered for you? If you have this sense of victory over sin and death, how would you describe it? What are some of the ways it can show itself in everyday behavior?

5) We speak of God's work as making mankind more human. Why do we need grace, if God simply wants us to become more human? Couldn't we become more human all by ourselves? Doesn't history suggest that men can become more and more human without God's help? Where, then, does God fit in the picture? For example, it is a fact that baptized people continue to commit sins. In general, they seem no more sensitive, human, or loving than the unbaptized. In what sense can we say that baptism effects a real change in a person?

6) This book spends practically no time in discussing sin in terms of reward and punishment. Do you find this disturbing? In your opinion, doesn't the discussion miss a significant point of Christian teaching by not developing sin in terms of reward and punishment? Or do you find this treatment of sin a more satisfying explanation of your experience?

7) Some people imply that sin is often a complex matter: even our good actions often have the taint of sin. Yet some Catholics feel that because of the clear and precise moral teaching of the Church, it is easy to know when and how a person sins or does good. Which of these approaches to sin seems closer to your personal experience? How would you talk about sin to a person whose experience is different from yours?

8) Do Catholics seem to be moving away from a preoccupation with the nature and seriousness of their sins? Do you think this is good or bad? Is it important to make a distinction between mortal and venial sins? How do you think people should approach the sacrament of Penance?

Salvation

The Impossible Dream

Despite hardship, deprivation, and despair, men keep on hoping and believing—again and again—that life will not disappoint them. This feeling of unquenchable hope is well expressed in the Broadway play, *Man of La Mancha.*

Don Quixote returns home at last after years of "knightly exploits." His housekeeper and his niece, embarrassed and humiliated by his ridiculous behavior, finally convince him that he is not really a knight, that all his chivalry was only buffoonery, that he is only a ridiculous old man. The force of this realization combines with the rigors of the past few years to put him on his deathbed. Sancho, his faithful "squire," ever at his side, is kept silent by Quixote's niece and her fiance.

Aldonza, the tavern wench whom Quixote had christened Dulcinea and revered as a great lady, bursts into the room. They try to restrain her. But she rushes to the side of the disheartened old man.

At first Quixote doesn't recognize her. "Try to remember," she pleads. "Try!"

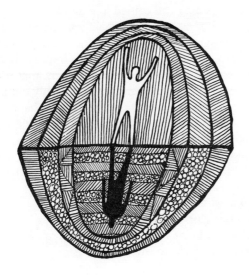

Slowly the old man comes to recognize the girl and realize what she is saying. "Perhaps it wasn't a dream!" he gasps, beginning to hope again. Suddenly he is transformed. He becomes the peerless Lord of La Mancha again. He struggles to his feet, calls to Sancho for his lance, and sweeps Dulcinea up off her knees. "My lady! It is not seemly!"

He begins to sing "The Impossible Dream":

> To dream the impossible dream,
> To fight the unbeatable foe,
> To bear with unbearable sorrow,
> To run where the brave dare not go,
> To right the unrightable wrong,
> To love pure and chaste from afar,
> To try when your arms are too weary,
> To reach the unreachable star,
> This is my quest . . .

Then he gasps and falls back onto his bed.

There is much that is overdone in this song, much that is maudlin. But somehow Don Quixote shines through. The Man of La Mancha was an ignorant old man, full of foolish superstitions and childish romantic dreams. He went out on a silly search that achieved almost nothing and caused him untold pain. Yet somehow Quixote lays hold of us. Somehow he shows us what it can mean to be human. He shows us what it is to dream an impossible dream, then reach out to possess it. He tells us what it means to believe that great ladies are to be found within tavern maids, that noble squires can be discovered in fat, stupid peasants, that silly old men are not useless dolts. He reveals humanity in the midst of banality, triviality, and shallow self-seeking. He tells men that the world is a valuable place, that life can be good, that it is a precious thing to be a man. He has a vision, however foolish and misguided, of what it means to become a man in the midst of a world in which true humanity seems only a dream.

> I know, if I'll only be true
> To this glorious quest,
> That my heart will be peaceful and calm,
> When I'm laid to my rest . . .

And the world will be better for this,
That one man, scorned and covered with scars,
Still strove with his last ounce of courage
To reach the unreachable star.

The God of the Future

Any questions raised about eschatology (what used to be called the "four last things") would, then, be not so much questions about the *end* of things as questions about the *future* — the future destiny of each man and, more important, of the entire people of the promise. Eschatology (study of the last things) therefore needs help from futurology (study of the future in the light of God's promises).

The word of God in the Old Testament, according to some theologians, is essentially a word of promise. And the transcendence, the "otherness" of God, is interpreted as linked with the future of mankind. One thing that makes God holy and transcendent is his Lordship over the future.

In the third chapter of the Book of Exodus, there is the famous passage where God speaks to Moses from the burning bush. God commands Moses to lead the people of Israel out of slavery. But Moses responds, "Who am I to go to Pharaoh and bring the Israelites out of Egypt? What shall I tell them is your name?" "I will be with you," God answers. According to many modern scholars, God's reply can be translated: "I will be who I will be." God sees himself as the God of the future. He is a God involved in human history and not simply a God existing above mankind in a kind of isolated heavenly sanctuary. He presents himself to Moses as one who intervenes in human history. And it is this God that draws the man of hope toward his destiny.

The man of Christian faith faces death and judgment with "joy set before him," as Christ did. Facing the critical moment of death and standing under God's judgment against his sin, the Christian relies on God's love, seen as a strong new thing — a transforming power in human history. The old horror of death is linked with God's promise of a new life and a new creation. And the world and each human life can be viewed as caught up in a single historical movement toward the fullness of God's promise.

The Promise of Salvation

How does Christian hope respond to God's promise of salvation?
Although sin, suffering, and death are clearly tied up with man's freedom and salvation, the Christian message is not a message about sin, suffering, and death. Rather it emphasizes the movement toward personhood and mature freedom in Christ. It concentrates on the mystery of salvation, the completion of God's work.

Salvation means different things to different people.

For some Christians, it means getting to heaven. They may think of heaven as a place where there is no work or where there is no pain and sorrow. Others see it as a refuge where men live close to God. Some even picture heaven as a quiet familiar home away from home where everyone will be completely at ease. Others make it something special — perhaps an idyllic, picturesque resort with ivory gates, ancient cobblestones, and melodious, golden-throated chimes. Others view heaven as a spare, monastic retreat where they will simply contemplate God for all eternity.

Though people describe heaven in different ways, each understanding of salvation and heaven represents someone's understanding of what is best and most important in the world, carried to the highest, most noble level of his imagination. And since heaven — or final salvation, however defined — is linked indissolubly with the good and perfect God, heaven itself must be a place in which the best things possible for human minds, hearts, and bodies are found.

Such an understanding of salvation is supported by the different ways the Bible discusses salvation. For Abraham and the early Israelites, who were nomads wandering in the desert in search of water, salvation meant a land "flowing" not just with water, but "with milk and honey." It meant numberless offspring so that one would be cared for in his old age and his name would not be forgotten.

On the other hand, the Israelites, after the division of the kingdom and David and Solomon, felt that the most perfect state was one in which a descendant of David would be appointed by God and once again establish the glory and power of the earlier kingdom. A slightly different view was held by some of the Israelites who were in Babylon in the second captivity after the temple had been destroyed by King Nebuchadnezzar. They saw salvation as freedom from bondage and restoration of the temple under a successor to David. Thus, throughout the Old Testament period, Israel talked about salvation in terms of current needs and desires.

Gradually, Israel began to see that salvation would never come through human achievement, wealth, military or political power. The Hebrew prophets began talking about God writing his law in men's hearts as the fulfillment of human life.

The first Christians were men and women who felt that God had worked a new and complete salvation in Christ. All the imperfections, distortions, and evil in the world would be taken up and transformed by what Christ had done.

The writers of the New Testament invoked many different images for salvation. Matthew saw it as the perfection of a new Israel, brought about by Jesus, the Messiah, in accordance with Jewish tradition. Paul saw Christ's salvation in many different ways. To him, Christ had broken down the wall of sin between men and God. He had justified us who were sinners. He had granted us eternal life.

In the years since Christ, men have seen salvation in still other ways. Pious and uneducated men often talk about it as if it were a place of plenty where all material wants will be satisfied. Some philosophers have viewed it as the human mind forever satisfied with the vision of God. Others emphasize the idea of unity with God.

All these different understandings of salvation and heaven show that no one is really sure what constitutes salvation. But we have some pointers. Salvation is when and where God and men live together as God intended. This relationship is characterized by love, openness, and freedom. Today people often talk about love as relating deeply to other people. A view of heaven in terms of personal relationships helps us understand many elements of revelation and heaven, but it is by no means a complete picture of salvation. For, as Paul says, there are things we have not yet seen.

In any case, salvation means that we will become what we were intended to be. It means that we will be fully human and transformed in his Spirit. It means that we will participate in God's love and that he will save us from whatever threatens us. This is what John means when he says that we already have eternal life insofar as we have begun to love, begun to be human, and begun to live in Christ. The unknown details of salvation are not really important. People have already begun to participate in salvation, and they can look forward confidently to its fulfillment, whatever form this may take.

In terms of God's salvation of mankind, how does the Christian of hope respond to the mysteries of death and judgment?

The Christian takes death and judgment seriously. For they remain for him an unexplained mystery, even in terms of God's promise of salvation.

There is no easy answer to the problem of death. Christians feel anxiety over death just as much as other people. When death appears, nothing can be said or done to make it easier. It is just there. Young men and women are cut down just as they are ready to start doing things. Children are carried away by childhood diseases. Parents are destroyed just when their presence seems most important to their children.

Yet there is another element in the Christian's response to death. It involves God's promise of salvation for mankind, the salvation that he is working now and will bring to completion at the Second Coming of Christ. Thus, in some manner, the Christian sees beyond what happens in history. He does not say: "Don't worry. Sin and death are conquered. Everything is really all right." His hope for the salvation of men is more complex than that: It recognizes the reality of death but sees beyond it.

Evil is real. In many instances, sin, evil, and death are clearly tied up with a person's free choice. An individual may freely choose to do something wrong. People may also recognize that they are somehow "infected" or "tainted" with evil in a way that they cannot really seem to grasp. They may feel a forceful, almost irresistible pull of evil. There also seems to be a mysterious element in the world — independent of men — which is destructive of humanity. The Bible speaks of this element as a group of "powers." Christians traditionally speak of Satan and his angels. But, however men try to picture this element, it seems clear that there is a malevolent force in the world that detours man and somehow shunts him aside from his goal of human growth in Christ.

The Christian tries to weave the facts of sin, evil, and death into his understanding of salvation, to create a realistic picture of what is going on in the world. His faith is that God is somehow still involved in working out the maturity and personhood of man and the humanity of the human race, even when it seems otherwise — even, in fact, in death. He believes that God in Christ has granted him leverage over suffering and death. He believes that "as he is made like Christ in his death, so he will be made like him in his resurrection."

What of judgment?

When a person realizes that a man may become "nothing," as Paul perceptively points out, this leads him to reach out for meaning, value, and security, to try to lay hold of anything that will guarantee life and meaning for him. But every attempt to capture some meaning is tied up at the same time in the general confusion and twistedness of things. For, as Paul says, by abandoning of their relationship with God, men separate themselves from the one who could grant life. Thus, they are seeking life in "creatures" rather than in the Creator God.

While men and women tend to move away from God, refusing his invitation to grow into the fullness of Christ, God is working out the salvation of mankind. His will is that all men be saved.

There are two schools of thought about how God has responded to this situation of salvation and sin. Both viewpoints see Christ as central to salvation. But they interpret his work differently.

The first view focuses on human freedom. God created man with the possibility of relating freely, openly, and lovingly. People could not really love God as personal beings (in the sense that God is personal) if they were only remote-controlled robots who went through the motions of relationships. For people to love God, they had to be given the option or possibility of not loving him.

This first view, then, holds that God did, in fact, create man with the freedom to reject him. It holds that Christ came to open to man the way to salvation and that he is not only redeemer of mankind, but its judge. Christ came to save men. But men can refuse to accept his saving power.

People in this group tend to talk about hell as the state of those who have chosen to reject God forever. Heaven is the place where those who chose salvation are united finally and fully with God.

The second view is conscious of the radical sinfulness of human nature and of the goodness of God. It takes very seriously what Paul says in the fourth chapter of Romans: "We were still help-

less when at the appointed time Christ died for sinful men . . ."
What proves that God loves us is that Christ died for us while we
were still sinners. Since he died to make us good men, he will not
fail to save us from God's wrath. This view holds that God will
ultimately save all men. The judgment which men experience is
their unavoidable and unstoppable spiral toward death. But already
in the book of Hosea, God's love for Israel despite its sins was expressed: ". . . the Lord gives his love to Israel though they turn to
other gods. . . . He will heal us . . . will bandage our wounds;
after a day or two he will bring us back to life, on the third day he
will raise us and we shall live in his presence." But God has proved
himself an utterly good and gracious God, who will not give men
over to destruction. He lovingly continues to work with them, sinful
as they are; he works with them toward their salvation. Though
this view speculates very little on the character of eternal life for
the unrepentant sinner, it is firm in faith in Christ — the belief that
"we shall be saved by him from the wrath of God."

Discussion

1) According to the discussion, the Christian of hope concentrates
on the mystery of salvation and the completion of God's work
rather than on considerations of sin, suffering, death. Is the Christian of hope in any way special? Haven't Christians always concentrated on hope and salvation? Weren't Christians always taught
such a sense of hope and confidence?

2) Discuss other people besides Don Quixote — in real life and
fiction — who have dreamed impossible dreams; e.g., Tom Dooley,
Doctor Zhivago, Thomas More. Does religion seem to be an element
in each dream? Is hope something optional in religion?

3) In the Bible God always seems to be active in the world:
leading his people somewhere, getting them out of trouble, promising them good things if they love and obey him. Does God seem
involved in human history today? Have you had any experiences you
would call experiences of God's power in the world today? What
were they? Does God really enter into men's lives?

4) If Christ conquered death, why must we all die? Is Christ concerned with a different sense of death than mere bodily death? Is it
possible to be dead while still physically alive? Does this have anything to do with the concept of mortal sin?

5) Few Christians talk publicly nowadays about heaven or life after death. How would you explain heaven to a child? To a grown-up who didn't believe in it? Does your idea of heaven reflect your personal values, or do you just use the definition of heaven you learned in the catechism? How does your idea of heaven compare with that of the people around you? How do Protestants think of heaven?

6) Are salvation and heaven the same thing? Can we say that our salvation has already begun on earth? In what sense?

7) Some theologians say that God will ultimately save every human person. Others say that every man has in himself the power to reject God for all eternity. Discuss each of the two approaches to salvation.

An opponent of the first position — that everyone will be saved — might ask the following questions: Don't you think that the idea of universal salvation would tend to nourish an immature and irresponsible attitude toward life? What meaning would sin and punishment for sin have in this theory? Doesn't it seem unjust (at least from a human point of view) that wicked and sinful people would receive the same reward as those who had worked all their lives at being good?

An opponent of the second position — that persons can reject God and choose hell — might ask: Doesn't this approach tend to fill us with an unchristian fear and dread rather than joy, enthusiasm, and openness in working to make the world more human? Doesn't this view also imply that God's almighty love is not really almighty, since it cannot save all men? Can a person in heaven ever be happy knowing someone he loves has rejected God forever?

Christ
the Pattern
of Hope

chapter 2

Understanding Jesus in History

Who Do Men Say that I Am?

"Gentle Jesus, meek and mild," sing little children in the third grade. "King of Kings and Lord of Lords," thunder the combined choruses of the city's colleges in public concert. "To Jesus' heart all burning," comes the song from a small group of ladies still faithful to Friday night benediction.

Throughout history billions of pictures of Jesus Christ have been produced and reproduced. Artists have tried to show what impressed them about Christ, or what their friends, their family or their own consciousnesses told them about him. They have turned out images in stone or wood, plaster or bronze, ivory or gold. Others have spoken of Christ in words, music, stone, and plastic.

There is a Jesus in tabernacles, in bibles, in art galleries, in history books, in sermons, in sculptures, in song, in legend, on Christmas cards, on movie screens, everywhere.

Among all the communications media, perhaps film is best able to deal with a complex and multifaceted subject like Christ. And motion picture producers have often tried, according to their limited lights, to create a comprehensive image of Jesus from all the factual material at hand. They have tried not to miss anything important. They have tried not to twist, bend, or distort.

Much truth. Much distortion. Like the strata of soil, there are layers of meaninglessness in all of these attempts.

The concept of Christ challenges and baffles the human mind. Images and impressions vary. There is Christ as human and Christ as divine. There is Christ sorrowing as he walks the streets of poverty and Christ who stands victorious for all mankind as Lord in power. "Who do you say that I am?"

Images of Jesus abound. Some images of Christ are clear, some hazy, some broken and shifting like a reflection in a rippling pond.

How can a person separate meaning from the meaningless, truth from distortion, light from darkness?

Christ's "titles" have created other layers of meaning and confusion. He is called Lord, Redeemer, Priest, Savior, King, Shepherd, Lamb, Word, Son of Man, Son of God, Messiah, Servant.

"Who do men say that I am?"

Perhaps we can at least reduce the confusion if we say what he is not. He is not a plastic luck charm. He is not an infant doll. He is not a December's Santa Claus. He is not a Divine Prisoner locked in ten thousand tabernacles. He is not a Cecil B. DeMille character. His name is not a taboo word or a curse. Yet people want positive knowledge. They ask: Who was this Jesus Christ? What is his role in history? What am I to think of him? What is his meaning for mankind?

How to Answer the Question

"Who is Jesus Christ?" What would a Catholic today answer? Perhaps he would be content to say simply: "Jesus Christ is the second person of the Blessed Trinity who became man in order to save men from sin." Or he might say that Jesus lived in a certain time and a certain place, and that no informed non-Christian would deny that this man lived in history. He might go on to tell about Christ's passion, death, and resurrection; and then explain how the risen Christ continues to give men his saving grace through the power of the Holy Spirit.

Do Catholics really have a single answer to the question, "Who is Jesus Christ?" Do any Christians?

There are about a billion Christians in the world, and about a half of them are Catholics. But whether Catholics or not, they all differ from each other in the millions of marvelous ways that human beings do. Some live in neat all-electric suburban homes, others in grass huts. Some are psychoanalysts, some nuclear physicists, some can't even read. Some follow their impulses, others live by a slide rule.

It is unlikely, then, that all these people think about Christ in the same way. A California farmer might not understand a Dutch theologian describing Christ as "the sacrament of the encounter with God." But the farmer — more than the theologian — would appreciate what Christ meant when he said: "I am the vine and you are the branches." The theologian should know ideas. The farmer may know vines. And each is happier and more confident talking about Christ in the words that are familiar to him.

The result of all these differences is that different men have different mental pictures and word images of Christ for people always try to picture who and what Jesus Christ is through the words and ideas closest to them. This doesn't mean that they deny there is one identical Jesus, "the God who became man in order to save us." It just means that people can't talk about Christ without using symbols and images that help them understand.

Images of Christ in the Bible

Each of the four evangelists paints a different portrait of Jesus Christ. *Mark's Gospel*, the earliest and most primitive, is simple in form. It begins with a vivid description of the deeds of Jesus during his public ministry, then spins out the plain story of the passion, death and resurrection of Jesus. Within the account of the ministry are three main themes or images of Jesus which come together in Jesus' death and resurrection. The first theme focuses on Jesus' travels through Galilee and Judea, where he teaches and works miracles. The second concentrates on the mounting hostility of priests, scribes and Pharisees toward him as they begin to suspect that he regards himself as the Messiah. The third theme centers on Mark's attempt to show that Jesus is, in fact, the Messiah. However, this is kept secret from all but a small group of followers.

Thus for Mark, there is Jesus as teacher and healer, Jesus the opponent of the Pharisees, Jesus the Messiah — three images.

Matthew's idea of Jesus is sharply different. While Mark tends to present Jesus' messianic role as real but deliberately hidden, Matthew wants to *proclaim* that he is indeed the royal Messiah of

David's line who will fulfill all the Old Testament promises. Over
and over again, Matthew quotes from the Old Testament to show
how Christ fulfills the promises. Christ is the Son of David. This
is why he was born in Bethlehem, the city of David. He is the suffering servant of the Lord promised in Isaiah 50 and 52. He is the
Emmanuel ("God with us") of Isaiah 7. He is the great teacher and
law-giver: a second Moses, who has come to the Jews not to destroy Moses' Law but to fulfill it. But all of these images in Matthew
are overshadowed by the broader, all-encompassing image of
the "kingdom of heaven" or reign of God which Christ has come
to establish. Christ is the Messiah, the king of his kingdom. But his
kingdom is not of this world.

Besides the historical side of Christ, Matthew stresses Jesus as
preacher and teacher. He gives a long and careful development of
the sermon on the mount. Matthew's Christ is famous for parables
and sermons, and even the miracles he reports are closely connected
with Jesus' teaching.

Luke emphasizes still other aspects. The Jesus he presents is
the Savior of *all* men — not just Jews. He is also the Lord of
universal mercy, and Luke's best parables — the lost sheep, the
prodigal son, the good Samaritan — focus on mercy and forgiveness. Luke's Jesus always practices the compassion he preaches. He
forgives the sinful woman who anoints his feet. He forgives
Zacchaeus the tax collector, forgives the people who have
crucified him, forgives the good thief who asks to be remembered
by him. Luke also works hard to show Jesus' love for the poor and
lowly in contrast to Jesus' criticism of the rich, especially those who,
in their pride, abuse their wealth. But in the parable of the barren
fig tree, Luke's Jesus shows his mercy even for the wicked. People
will not be condemned until they've had a fair chance to repent,
he says. For Jesus deeply loves mankind, and he weeps over Jerusalem, although he knows its people are about to put him to death.

John presents still another side of Jesus. His Jesus evokes mysterious images that strongly suggest his divinity. In John, Jesus is
the light that conquers darkness, the word of God made flesh, the
word who comes from God and pitches his tent among men.

In his various letters, *Paul* develops whole new sets of ideas to
preach Jesus as *Lord* and *Christ*. This is Christ crucified and risen —
Christ who destroys the wall of hostility that separates man from

man. Christ is the second Adam who brings man goodness, maturity and life just as the first Adam brought man sin and death. He is the man emptied of his Godhead, suffering and dying for us. He is the firstborn of all creation. He is the love of God made visible. He is the power of God, the wisdom of God.

The Epistle to the Hebrews sees Christ as the new high priest, the mediator between God and man who has replaced the Jewish high priest of the temple.

In some ways, the most fascinating images of all come from the Apocalypse — the Book of Revelation. Here is how Christ is described in Revelation 19 as he comes to battle with the forces of evil:

"Then I saw heaven opened, and behold, a white horse! He who sat upon it is called Faithful and true, and in justice he judges and makes war. His eyes are like a flame of fire, and on his head are many diadems; and he has a name inscribed which no one knows but himself. He is clad in a robe dipped in blood, and the name by which he is called is the Word of God. . . . From his mouth issues a sharp sword with which to smite the nations, and he will rule them with a rod of iron; he will tread the wine press of the fury of the wrath of God the Almighty. On his robe and on his thigh he has a name inscribed: King of Kings and Lord of Lords."

Jesus' Meaning in History

What is the meaning of the Jesus who lived in history for the Christian of today? What can we know of Jesus of Nazareth as he actually was?

Any discussion about Jesus in history must take into account varying levels of importance. What is most important, of course, is the meaning and purpose of his life on earth, rather than facts about his personality, actions, and teachings (though these, of course, are also important).

After more than one hundred years of New Testament historical research, and after many shifts of opinion, the consensus of scholars is that an accurate historical biography of Jesus can never be written, because there is not enough data for such a biography. The writers of the Gospels were concerned with *preaching the good news of the risen Christ, not with presenting his historical biography*. Crucial sources for our knowledge of Jesus in history are the four Gospels. There are a number of apocryphal Gospels in existence, but they are of little historical merit. The Acts of the Apostles, the letters of Paul and other apostles, and other New Testament writings put Jesus in a central position, yet give few if any further historical clues about his life.

The purpose of the New Testament authors, then, was not to write a life of Jesus, but to give an account of Christ's life and teaching in the light of the needs of the growing Christian communities. Even the personality of Jesus, it seems, was not the writers' primary interest.

A year-by-year account of Jesus' life can be built only along broad, general lines. Even the exact dates of his birth and death cannot be determined, though most scholars believe that his life falls roughly between the death of Herod (4 B.C.) and A.D. 30.

The three synoptic Gospels (Matthew, Mark, Luke) agree on no more than a general scheme of Jesus' public life. There was his baptism by John, the temptation, the preaching in Galilee, the journeys to Jerusalem, a brief period of teaching in Jerusalem, and finally his passion, death, and resurrection. Scholars estimate the length of his public ministry at between one and three years.

But just as a biography of Jesus cannot be written, so it is almost impossible to outline a synopsis of his teaching. The primitive Christian community, in its early period, made no attempt to isolate the teaching of Jesus from its own teaching. The apostles saw themselves as empowered by Jesus to carry on and develop his teaching. The principal element in his teaching and theirs was Jesus himself.

To repeat, the only biographical material we have is the Gospels; and they are nothing more than the written version of what was taught by the primitive Church. The primitive Church got its teaching from (1) its memory of the life, person, and teaching of Jesus; (2) its reflections about the meaning of the gospel; and (3) new problems which were raised from time to time about the substance of Christian faith.

In treating Jesus as a historical person, the theologian tries to do the same thing as the evangelists. He is not out to capture all the details of Jesus' life and personality, but to present him in terms of Christian faith and preaching. Thus to the theologian of hope, Jesus Christ is *re-creator of the world.* Jesus was Messiah, savior, prophet, and priest of the new covenant. But above all he was and is *Lord.*

New Testament writings show him to be a divine person, the Son of God the Father. God's original creation was "very good," but it became twisted and perverted by evil. *The task of Jesus was to "re-create" the world*, to lead a revolt against its perversion and distortion.

So Christian hope sees Jesus as standing out from the world in full possession of the only power that can save it. He displayed that divine power in his resurrection from the dead; for he defeated death, the greatest evil of all. And Christians believe that since Jesus conquered death, he can conquer any evil.

When Jesus rose from the dead, then, he gave men the hope that someday, somehow, all the world's evil would be conquered as completely as he had conquered death. And he continues to inspire that hope through the work of the Holy Spirit in the Church. "What the Spirit produces is love, joy, peace, patience, kindness, goodness, faithfulness, gentleness, self-control."

Thus Christian hope stresses man's role in Christ's continuing revolt against the conquest of evil. Jesus' resurrection is assurance that God is embarked on a project for man's future — to wipe all evil from the face of the earth. Man's own plans and projects are of great value, but they are still less than perfect, since the good and true hopes of men are often infected with evil. Consequently, mankind may be frequently asked to discard its own notions of the way the future should be and prepare for the future that God is fashioning.

Discussion

1) Do you find it upsetting that we shall probably never have a completely certain historical account of the life and teachings of Jesus? Why or why not?

2) The Gospels read at Mass on Sundays relate the actions and teachings of a man who understood and spoke to a world that is two thousand years gone. What do these readings have to do with present-day life? Do you sometimes feel that priests in their sermons often use the words of Jesus as a convenient starting point for "grinding their own axes"? Can a priest or anyone else really translate Christ's life and miracles into a form which has something to do with the life of modern men?

3) Have you ever noticed how many images of Jesus there are

in the Gospels: high priest, savior, Word of God made flesh, lamb
of God, son of man, son of God, good shepherd, and many more?
Does it help you to distinguish these various images of Christ, or do
you just find most of them confusing and without any clear meaning? Do you find any of these images more attractive than others?
Why?

4) Jesus' death and resurrection are the central points of the
Christian mystery. In growing up a Catholic, were you made to feel
the fundamental importance of Christ's resurrection from the dead?
In your experience, do the various ceremonies and devotions of
the Church (novenas, the stations of the cross, vigil lights, the rosary,
medals, devotion to the Blessed Mother and the saints, sermons, religious books and magazines, and the rest) emphasize or detract
from the central mysteries of Christ's death and resurrection?

The Christ of the Present:
Person and Power

New Testament teaching on salvation emphasizes that Christ —
once he achieved man's redemption through his own death and
resurrection — returned to the Father. This passage from the Father

and, through the human condition, back to the Father has been a favorite theme of Christian writers.

But precisely because of this passage to the Father, the Christian living after Christ's time is confronted with a major problem. Though he accepts the fact that the Holy Spirit was sent to tell him of the work of Christ, he still feels the need for some image or view of Christ that will guide him in his conduct and encourage him in his faith.

So the central question confronting the Christian has been: "What think you of Christ? How do you imagine him, how do you understand him?" One can almost say: "Show me your image of Christ, and I will tell you what you are all about, and what you are trying to become."

Two Kinds of Answers

If someone asked American Catholics what Christ meant in their lives, their answers would probably fall into two groups. These groups are not opposed to one another, but they strongly emphasize two different aspects of the reality of Christ.

In varying degrees, one group would feel a sense of Christ as personal friend, brother, and intimate companion. They feel that Christ, while at the Father's right hand, is also really and effectively *present as a companion to men*, in their dealings with others, in the world in which they live. They believe he is with them *personally*, not as an abstract moral model or visionary's dream. He is their friend, their own Savior, the Jesus who knows their weaknesses "because he himself was subject to weakness." In reading Scripture or hearing about Christ in the Gospel during Mass, they sense Christ as intimately present *now*. He encouraged, healed, taught, cajoled, worried and loved when he was among men in the flesh. He continues to do all these things now as well.

The second group does not deny Christ's personhood and his glorified *humanity*. But it accents not friendship but Paul's view of Christ as *divinely powerful*: Christ the breaker of the power of sin, victor over dissolution and death, and the power of the present age. This group sees Christ as opening up the possibilities of freedom, reconciliation, and fulfillment for all men. It sees Christ as powerful, as the source of men's strength and ability to become more human — more like what God intends man to be. Christ's resurrection and ascension have placed him beyond the limited vision of personality we have. And without becoming an abstract life-force in men's lives, he has become, through his conquest of death, the risen one who is Lord of history. The Christian draws his understanding of Christ from the testimony of Scripture, tradition, and the interior witness of the Holy Spirit. This testimony is extremely rich in different kinds of images. But why is one image or a whole group of images chosen over others? The reasons are complex, and they reflect the wide variety of temperaments, mentalities, cultures, and epochs that have affected the history of the Christian Church. Faced with the criticisms of pagan philosophers, some early apologists saw Christ in terms of God's Reason or Mind. Martyrs and persecuted peoples found inspiration in the image of Christ as the suffering and crucified Son of God. The Middle Ages saw him as Lord and King, the "Enlightenment" as an outstandingly moral man. The twentieth century has seen Christ as *Man*, as *the* man for others. But none of these images grasps the whole reality of Christ. Each tries to point to a dimension, an aspect — an intriguing, but limited facet.

As we have already suggested, it is possible to group the different images of Christ around two cores, without setting one group against the other. We might call them the human or "personal" and the divine or "power" images.

The Christian who views Christ as friend and personal savior selects elements from the synoptic portrayals of him. Christ related to other people in various ways and was especially close to the disciples and certain followers. Some of the apostles even received his special affection — Peter and John, for example, and he was a close friend of Lazarus and his sisters. People watched him smile and grow angry. They touched him and his clothes. They acted and he responded. He stood on the ground or sat at a table, expressed his feelings and answered questions. He lived and acted as a compassionate person, a man among men. He related to people as a man. Christians with a "personal" image of Christ recognize that he is now the Risen Lord. But they also feel that he is still a personal friend; and it is as a personal friend that they pray to him, think of him, love him, and "live in him."

The scriptural understanding of Christ as "power" has strong roots in Paul's image of him. For Paul, Christ is the power of salvation in the Gospel. He is "Christ the power of God and the wisdom of God." By faith, men win "the knowledge of Christ, the power of his resurrection." When persecuted, men are asked to put their belief in the power of God who raised Christ from the dead. Paul speaks of living in Christ, dying and rising with Christ. But this is not the sense of personal friendship discussed above. Paul realizes that the personhood of Christ goes far beyond the "gentle Jesus, meek and mild." He realizes that Christ is the risen Lord and cannot be contained in all-too-human modes of thinking.

Theologians Look at the Images

The contemporary theologian sees both strengths and weaknesses in each of the two images of Christ.

One basic advantage to the "personal friend" image is that its vividness and "personality" enables many people to feel that Christianity is a religion of personal participation and concern. There is a sense of God's personal concern for each human being. And this concern gives "heart" to God's infinite, unimaginable love. It counterbalances the Catholicism anchored to formulas and propositions which have been a major preoccupation for Catholics.

Some think there is a second advantage. They argue that early Christians often chose to emphasize Christ's *humanity*, portraying him in his earthly life as a man among men. They also argue that the evangelists emphasized Christ's humanity.

But other biblical scholars feel that the evangelists were primarily concerned to show that Jesus' human life, death, and resurrection were *redemptive signs*, pointing to the coming kingdom of God. Perhaps their response helps explain why it is so hard to make a good film about Christ. It would be tremendously difficult to make a movie about the man who was revealed as redeemer of all mankind — and yet lived in a little backward province in the far corner of the Roman Empire. If the movie presents him realistically, it dresses him up in strange clothing and has him speak in proverbs.

Paul suggested that the real scandal of Christianity is that the only begotten Son of God should become a *man* — be born of a woman, be raised through childhood, and die a human death. As Paul says, there is no way the wisdom of the Greeks could grasp such a thing. And perhaps this means that there is no way people can make a realistic and authentic movie about Jesus.

But there is a danger also that one's image of Christ can too easily be modelled on personal sentimentalism and thus verge on idolatry. Or Christ can become a purely human "good guy," an easy ethical model, who "justifies" a person's own view of the ideal order. Christ, for example, can be viewed as someone who approves, rather than challenges, many of the assumptions of a twentieth century Catholic. It is too easy to want a "meaningful Christ" — but one who does not demand more than a fairly simple code of behavior. Christ becomes no more than "my better self," which is a kind of blasphemy.

Also, the personal approach can limit Christ's relation to the Christian as that of a "friend," thus enabling the Christian to ignore the reality of the rest of the world. Christ and the world can be made to exist in separate spheres. And the Christian may be encouraged to split his life into one area where Christ related to him and another where he does not. Christianity can then become a narrow and sentimental individualism.

An example of this sentimental and "humanized" view of Jesus may be seen in many of the pictures of the Sacred Heart. One particularly romantic rendering shows Jesus standing with his heart in one hand and his other hand outstretched to offer solace to the observer. His face is soft and effeminate. His hair falls in long curly ringlets about his shoulders and shines as if it had just been shampooed. His clothes are draped in soft folds and seem to be made of some incredibly silky material. Around his head are little sparkles of light, while a ring of light surrounds his heart. The heart itself is surmounted by a tiny cross and tinier tongues of fire. The whole picture seems intended to convey some kind of close and intimate relationship with Christ. It is bathed in a sentimental nostalgia, glowing with an unearthly sort of radiance.

It is difficult to see how such a Christ could have anything to do with social issues, with ghettos, jobs, politics, schools, and stores. He is almost completely cut off from the present-day world of experience. His function seems to be to make one feel good, to make one feel that Jesus is his friend and cares about him. There is intimacy here. Invitation and an offer of friendship. But the soft, radiant figure is too sweet for comfort.

Some Christians, then, see Christ very possessively — as *My* Lord and *my* God! The idea that Christ has to do with economics, politics, science, or international relations would seem strange to them.

The second basic image of Christ has a great deal of strength. It is the image of Christ as victor over the power that twists and distorts human life. It expresses Paul's conviction that the point for the Christian is not to know Christ in the flesh, but to know Christ in the power of the Spirit. This indeed is the vocation of all men living out Christ's resurrection. And it has been suggested, as well, that Paul's view provides a broad background, neither too vague nor too specific, for interpreting what God desires for men, both in worldly and in spiritual matters. It is also far less open to the dangers of sentimental individualism.

Its primary shortcoming is that a Christian may become excessively intellectual and "cosmic" in his view of Christ. In a word, Christ can become a *function* of one's world-view, and thus become impersonal. If the Christ of power is separated from Christ as person, something of the full reality of Christ is lost.

An example of this kind of excessive abstraction and impersonality can be seen in much Byzantine art. Though very valuable the Orthodox emphasis on Christ's role in "divinizing" men led many Byzantine artists to a real neglect of his humanity. He is understood as being far away, infinitely beyond men: an abstract judge and a majestic, kingly, figure who doesn't seem to be human at all. He seems to have little or nothing to do with the situation of ordinary human beings. And people need to know Christ is concerned about people. They need to know that he is not just far away on a throne of glory.

Discussion

1) In your own experience, how do people find meaningful ways of relating to Christ? Have you found a relation in your own life to the reality of Christ?

2) Prayer seems to be a significant way of relating to Christ. Why do we have so many different forms of prayer: prayers with set words like the Lord's Prayer and the prayers at Mass, and spontaneous prayers and prayers of silent meditation? Wouldn't Christian life be more alive and spontaneous if it did away with most kinds of formal prayer? Isn't an individual's relationship to Christ a very personal thing, a thing which the formalities of religion can only hinder?

3) Can the parish structure provide genuine assistance in developing a personal relationship to Christ?

4) The book discusses two basic ways in which people see Christ relating to them. Some people see him primarily as a person: as friend, companion, model of behavior. Others see him chiefly as the almighty power which continues the work of saving man despite man's sins and failure.

If we think of Christ as a person, isn't there a temptation to create fantasy, to dream up an image of someone who is not really there as a living human being is — one we can hear, see, touch? Isn't it rather phony to call one-sided praying to Christ a "conversation" with him? On the other hand, didn't all the saints think of Christ as a person and a personal friend?

If we think of Christ as a power, how can a human person have a loving relationship with someone he knows only as an abstract force or power, especially when the relationship a man seeks with Christ concerns very personal and human matters: sickness, repentance, success, peace, happiness, death, hope? On the other hand, doesn't it seem more realistic to think of Christ as a power, since we cannot physically sense his presence in our lives?

5) The book says: "show me your image of Christ and I shall tell you what you are like and are trying to become." Among the people you know (including yourself), is this in any way true? Even if it is, does it really say anything about Christ or your relation to him?

6) Different images of Christ have been popular at different times in history. Is our own age characterized by any special image of Christ? Or several images? Discuss them. Are they healthy images? Merely commercialized? Think, for example, of the plastic dashboard Jesus, the painting of the Sacred Heart, the statue of the Infant of Prague. How do the images we are most attracted to reflect our understanding of Christ? How do we see Christ in relation to the Christian community?

Christ and Tomorrow

Looking at Tomorrow

"Instead of working for the improvement and conquest of the earth, wouldn't it be better to abandon to its own sort of suicide this absurd world which destoys its own best productions, and preoccupy oneself with the supernatural alone . . . ?"

Does the man who wrote these words sound cynical, discouraged, bitter? Could he be a Christian who loves men and the world? Could he value technology? Could he be a dedicated scientist? A theologian of hope? A priest preoccupied with the shaping of mankind's future? The answer to these questions is "yes." He is all of them. The words are from a letter written in 1916 from the battlefront by the Jesuit Pierre Teilhard de Chardin. Teilhard's friend, Boussac, had just been killed at the front. He had been taken from Teilhard's life; and Teilhard's first reaction — like a knee reflex — was to reject everything he and Boussac had ever hoped for. All Teilhard saw was that this absurd world had destroyed Boussac, "one of its own best productions, one of the pillars of my future."

In time, however, the spirit of hope reasserted itself, and Teilhard returned to work with renewed vigor. He was determined to place his faith in the "reality of spirit and its survival," and never

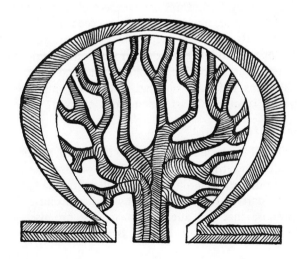

waver in his effort to shape the earth. He would never give up hope.

At one time or another, the world offers every man encouragement or discouragement, certainty or doubt, failure or success.

At one time or another in his life, everyone feels the power of the world to discourage and oppress. The student who flunks an exam, the salesman who sees doors slammed in his face, the research scientist who cannot come up with the right solution. The actress who can't get a break. The father of a growing family who has no hope for a raise in pay. The businessman with a hot new idea, but no way to cut through the corporate red tape that strangles him. A moment of forgetfulness, of spite, of hesitancy, of over-eagerness — all of these trying little moments can dash to the ground our best laid plans.

But in all these plights there sometimes appears a light of human hope, something that gets us to look toward possibilities. A widow puts away her clothes of mourning; a student prepares again for the exam he failed; the husband and wife try again to have another baby after a miscarriage, or keep looking for a better apartment, or try to find a way out of their staggering money problems.

There are feelings of trust and sorrow, contrition and forgiveness that look to a richer life in the future. The desire to grow and understand looks with hope to the future. The interest in new experiences, new pleasures, new challenges, new relationships points to the future.

Sometimes strong friendships and respect can grow out of the deepest dislike. Handicapped people can succeed in many fields of life, despite the loss of an arm, a leg or their precious eyesight. Many poor people manage to break out of their slums. Sometimes men can open their eyes to the world of possibility, and find hope.

Can Christians rightfully say that whenever genuine hope for human growth is found, Christ is somehow involved?

The Future of Jesus Christ

In the biblical understanding of reality as history, the arrows are always pointing toward the future. The Bible pictures man as living within the framework of promise and fulfillment. The spectacle of sin the early part of Genesis gives way to the promise of Abraham, a promise that will affect all men. The promise of God's help and protection is accorded all the Israelites after their passage from Egypt. David is a lad "taken from the pasture," who will have a name equal to that of the greatest name. And in a dark hour for Israel, when kingdom and nationhood are only memories, God promises Israel "new things, secret and unknown," a new Jerusalem, a new people, a new creation.

Christ comes into the world of man and sin and begins to fulfill God's promises. Christian faith lives out of the resurrection of Jesus — the first-born of the new creation. This faith is directed in hope toward the universal future of Jesus Christ. This is not just any future, but the future of Jesus Christ.

In faith, Christians can see that the future *belongs* to Christ and will come about, finally, by the power of God's action in Christ. Nevertheless, men can hope and work for the future in a way that is meaningful. The future of man will not, however, simply be the work of man with an "assist from God." The full future of man will come when God brings history to an end and becomes "everything to everyone." Thus the object of the Christian's hope is the final consummation of the divine plan.

The Christian may see Christ in the "image" of a person or a power. What is essential, in any case, is the common hope that animates and guides him. Hope points him beyond his present accomplishments and beyond his sins to the promises that God has made in Christ. These promises bear with them the power to break down the sinfulness of the present and open it to future fulfillment.

The "personal" Christ focuses the Christian's attention on the personal, healing events in men's lives. These events testify to the entrance of God's power into the world. A leper is cured, a blind man sees, the hungry are fed, the bereaved find joy, the sinner is forgiven, the fearful are encouraged. The Christ of the synoptic Gospels announced the coming of the reign of God. But this reign never remained abstract and vague. Jesus was a personal sign pointing to the transformation that God was going to bring about in the world.

Christ as power focuses on the total universe, on the whole of history. And this Christ can never be plucked out of the air, pinned down, and labelled like some rare butterfly mounted on a board ("Here is the Messiah, there is the Messiah!"). The plan is God's, the power is God's, the future is God's in that it is Christ's. Men are to share in that Christ, his power, and his future, but they are always recipients. The gift of sharing in God's redeeming, liberating, and humanizing work is given to man, not seized by him. This is the Christ of John's Gospel, the Christ of Paul's preaching, the Christ whose rule will be definite, specific, universal, and divine — "not made with hands," not of human creation.

The Difference It Makes

One of the crucial questions that faces a theologian is the Christian's relationship to Christ in faith, hope, and love.

What difference does it make to be a Christian, living in the Spirit of Christ, believing in the power of his redemptive death and resurrection?

Modern theologians, much more than their predecessors, emphasize the universal importance of Christ's redemption. All men are living, and have always lived, in a world created and redeemed by God in Christ. All live in a "graced" world. There is no denying that our world is also a broken world. But it is being redeemed as well. God's grace abounds in all the world, in all men. Theologians such as Karl Barth and Karl Rahner have discussed the sense in which all men — pagan, agnostic, atheist, Mohammedan, Jew, Christian — share in Christ's redemption, whether they live in a situation of belief or unbelief or even if they have never heard of Jesus Christ.

If the Christian recognizes God's action as penetrating and enveloping all of human history, what does the explicit acceptance of Christ mean? What does explicit involvement in the visible Christian community mean? To one person, it might seem to be a complication of life. Another person might find it superfluous, or an unnecessary luxury. A third person might look upon his belief in Christ as a way to escape from ordinary life, from "the foolishness of this world." Someone else might see Christianity as the context in which to make basic life decisions. Perhaps some even see the Church as the place where the real drama of human life is played out.

Another point made by contemporary theologians puts a sharp edge on the question. Nothing is guaranteed to the Christian simply by his act of belonging to the visible community of the Church. Moreover, his explicit Christian commitment does not render him saved or more "saveable" than other men. Rather, a man's decision to be a Christian is his attempt to bear witness to what God is doing in the world and to be of some service in God's recreation of the world: This is the task of the man who is becoming human in and through Christ. The Christian is aware that God is acting among men and has promised men a future. This is the "good news" at which no philosophy and no merely human reflection can arrive. And Christians feel that it needs telling, because too often people think about giving up on the whole human project. Christians believe that this promise God made to all men in Christ has crucial significance for man's future. It is significant because it is the sign and promise of the seriousness with which God regards the future of mankind.

Discussion

1) When are people most likely to turn to Christ? Is it only when they are discouraged, depressed, failing — or also when they are happy, involved, hopeful? Do you know people who derive a certain zest and enthusiasm for life from their own particular image of Christ?

2) What part does man's work play in shaping the future? Sometimes the book seems to suggest that what man does or fails to do is very important. At other times it seems to suggest that things are in God's hands and no one else's. Can these two ideas be reconciled?

3) If we take a realistic look at the last two thousand years, how can anyone say that sin and death have been overcome by the resurrection of Christ? Do you think the Christian of the 1970's has a better right than previous generations to claim that sin and death are being overcome? Do you sense from your own experience of life that sin and death are being overcome in the modern world?

4) If all men live in a world created and redeemed by God, what is the value in being a Christian? What are some of the ways in which people you know find significance in being a Christian? Do Catholics — or even Christians — have a monopoly on God's grace?

Part II
THE PEOPLE OF THE PROMISE

The People
and
the Spirit

chapter 3

Discovery of the Spirit

Wonder and Gift

For some people, life is one big circus-tent of wonders. Just around the bend, new marvels and new surprises beckon — some good, some bad. All of the wonders, which James Joyce, the great Irish novelist, liked to call "epiphanies," make us what we are. Some people see only the dark side of experience: creeping socialism, galloping inflation, the specter of atomic annihilation, riots, crime, air pollution, people in the neighborhood who play their stereos too loud. These people move like sulky planets through the troubling, hostile universe of life. Others marvel at the brighter things, the wonders: a baby's first step, a golden afternoon, a wild ride down winding streets, a fantastic skyscraper, an incredibly happy marriage.

The difference between the two groups is that the person who has not lost his child-like capacity for wonder does not take life for granted. He continues searching for something creative, challenging, and illuminating in his varied world of people, things, and sensations. He is "hipped" on life; he is absorbed with events around him, with the currents of his existence, with the entire miracle of being alive. Like the English poet Edward Young, he feels that "Nothing, but what astonishes, is true."

Two boys stroll side by side down a bright, sunny street. One points to something on the other side of the road. They look at one another and laugh. Together, they run across the street. They are friends, and they know it. Out of the rich soil of their youth and imagination has sprung a relationship, a vital contact.

A boy and a girl are in love. In the stream of their shared experience, each comes to understand more about what it means to be alive, to be together.

Two proud young parents look lovingly at their new baby. They see a unique and individual person, a whole new life drawn from their love, something that came into the world because of them and through them, yet is beyond them. The child is the precious mirror of their existence. They see themselves in the color of his eyes and hair, the shape of his nose. He will for a time take on their mannerisms, and later develop his own unique set of responses. The child is part of them, and yet different. He is woven into the fabric of their love and thoughts and dreams; he is one with them, yet somehow separate. This is the experience of human unity, the inspiration behind W. H. Auden's touching line, "We must love one another, or die."

To the people who see and savor the wonder of living, all this is very much like receiving a gift. The gold paper and red ribbon speak an exciting language all their own. Someone cares. Someone has taken time. Someone values us. This is important all by itself, no matter what is inside.

To take part in friendship, love, loyalty, and understanding is to share a gift which brings value and rich new dimensions into one's portion of the world. Individuals — especially those with hope and vision — see and experience the gifts and wonders which grow out of many other human situations. Some recognize gifts of truth in a scientific research team hot on the trail of a new medical discovery. Some find them in a group of bright young college men meeting at a professor's home for a free-wheeling discussion. Some see gifts of life in a young executive who, when given a free hand, doubles his output, or in a talented student when he meets a great teacher who can alter the whole course and concept of his life.

By gaining such experience, Christians discover the Spirit of God alive and at work in the world. The Spirit's work is to help people grow through love into the fullness of Christ, to expand the dimen-

sions of living among individuals and societies, to open new high-
ways to truth, knowledge, and understanding, and to unclog the
lines of communication among persons and nations. By recognizing and responding to the meaning, value, and wonder of experience, we come to discover that, as Chesterton put it in *Orthodoxy*,
"The world is a wild and startling place." This is the excitement of
the Spirit.

The Spirit As Person

In the Old Testament, the Spirit of God signified "God's breath,"
his life-giving power; it was as active and effective as God himself.

The ancient world looked upon breath as a mysterious powerful,
and terrifying force. Sometimes it was gentle, sometimes violent.
But it was always a source of life and strength which men could
neither exhaust nor duplicate.

The breath or Spirit of God was a power affecting one's mind.
In the Old Testament, the Spirit of God was a divine power that
gave the prophets insight into God's purpose. It inspired the writers
of sacred books and gave strength to men who needed great courage.
In other passages, God's Spirit is conceived more as a teacher or
a guide, the source of all intellectual and spiritual gifts, and as a
force bestowed on certain individuals — for example, Moses,
Joshua, David, and particularly the promised messianic king whom
the Jewish nation awaited.

The chief signs of God's future covenant would, according to the
Old Testament, include a religious and moral transformation of all
mankind. So the prophets — and Isaiah in particular — frequently
spoke of God's Spirit bringing about this transformation in the coming new age. Not only the community, but every individual would
be morally re-created by the Spirit of God.

In the New Testament God's Spirit is a sanctifying power.

At Jesus' baptism the descent of the Holy Spirit symbolized God's
anointing and choosing of Jesus: His work began under the sign
of the Spirit.

This baptism marked the beginning of the moral and religious
re-creation of the people of the new covenant which the prophets
had promised. The outpouring of this Holy Spirit at the first Christian Pentecost was a sign for the apostles that the kingdom of God
was coming, and that Jesus who had given power to them from

heaven was revealing his royal power at the right hand of the Father.

In the New Testament there is a gradual revelation that the Spirit of God is a person. For John, the Holy Spirit is the Spirit of truth, and "another helper." The Spirit is another helper because, after Christ's ascension, he guides and directs the disciples. He reveals Christ to them, recalls to their minds what he had taught them, gives testimony concerning Jesus and glorifies him.

One in Hope

What did the Holy Spirit do in the lives of the early Christians? Of what importance is the early Christian community to us? What is the relationship of the work of the Holy Spirit to that of Jesus?

The early Christian community in Jerusalem was given its attitude or direction of life by the Spirit. The community was often portrayed as a kind of inclusive group — (though a deeply personal and human one), but its main purpose was outward and directed toward the future. The Spirit's work among early Christians was to help them give witness to the resurrection of Christ.

The essential unity of the early Christian community is founded on its hope in the saving activity of God among men, guaranteed by Jesus' resurrection and reaffirmed in the work of the Spirit among them. The unity of the early Christians also pointed toward the future in terms of the community's hope for the coming of the Lord — the eschatological event. According to its understanding of Jesus' promise, the community believed this coming was to occur very soon.

Aside from this essential unity of faith and hope, signs in the New Testament suggest that the early Christian community was made up of people with widely varying views. Some believed in Christ as Paul described him, others according to Mark's description; still others followed John's or James' understanding of him. They believed in one Lord (but many acceptable images), one Christ (but many theologies about him), one Church (but many different understandings of it). Some continued to participate in the rituals of Israel. Some formed their own ritual. Some abstained from food offerings to idols, others did not. Still others were circumcised, and others not.

The new Christians grew out of the Jewish tradition, but were transformed by the new thing God had done. The Spirit made real in their lives what God had accomplished for them in Christ. They were united in the faith that Jesus was the Messiah, the fulfillment of God's promise, and in the hope that Jesus would come to complete his new creation.

The Spirit's work is to complete the work of Jesus. Jesus called the Holy Spirit his Spirit, and the early Christians often thought of the Spirit as the effective presence of Christ in their midst.

Christ is the firstborn of a new creation. The early Christians saw him as the new Adam calling to them from the future to join in this new creation and grow into full personhood. To achieve the maturity of Christ among believers and to ready them for the return of the Lord, the Spirit poured himself out upon them continually and in ever new ways. He enriched their faith in Jesus, strengthened their hope in God's promises, and filled their lives — individually and as a community — with the love of Jesus, their redeemer.

Like their early counterparts, modern-day Christians hear Christ calling to them from the future. And today, as in the days of the early Christians, it is the love of Christ that ultimately unites Christians. They are united in the faith that he is sending the Spirit to transform the lives of men and the world they inhabit; they are united in the hope that he will one day come again in glory as Lord to take them and all mankind to himself.

Discussion

1) We often seem to talk about the work of the Holy Spirit on the human level: nourishing friendship, family love, politeness, courtesy, thoughtfulness, and so on. Yet Catholics have always been taught that the Holy Spirit's work is supernatural. How do you explain the apparent contradiction? Can there be a Christian dimension in the experience of modern technology and progress? It seems that natural science, psychology, and sociology — without the help of religion — adequately explain modern progress. Why does Christian hope stress the work of the Spirit in this area?

2) Do you have a personal image of the Holy Spirit? Do you picture him, for example, as wind or breath? As teacher or guide? As a force you can feel in your own life but can't quite describe? What role do you see the Holy Spirit playing in your life? What does it mean to say that the Spirit's work is to help human beings grow through love into the fullness of Christ?

3) Love for one another is said to be the chief sign of the members of the Christian community. How then do Christians explain the fact that many Christians disagree with one another, become embittered with one another, even fight and kill one another? At the same time, how do Christians explain the many non-Christian and even non-religious groups which are noted for the love their members show for one another? Must we look elsewhere than "loving one another" for the essential sign of Christian community?

4) We see Jesus bringing about a new creation and the Spirit carrying on Jesus' work. What does this new creation mean? Is it just a new word for "salvation" or "heaven"? Or does the expression mean something different? The power of the Spirit seems to be building a new creation on earth today. Are there any signs of this? Does the human race seem to be growing in a new way? In any way? Are there any ways in which the past ten or twenty years have been especially hopeful?

5) This book speaks a great deal of Christ's second coming. Is a sense of expectancy for the coming of Christ part of the Catholic tradition in recent centuries? Does talking about the second coming add anything to our experience of Christianity? Do people feel that the second coming is so far off that it is misleading and a waste of time to emphasize it? If we await Christ's second coming, in what ways is our waiting different from the waiting of the early Christians, who expected Christ to come almost immediately?

Discovery of Community

They Were United

Will Protestants and Catholics ever get together permanently?

Recently the people of a Presbyterian church in an integrated urban area invited a Catholic priest and some of his parishioners to celebrate Mass in their church. The Catholic bishop approved and so they went. However, one thing worried the Catholic priest. That was the problem of allowing the Protestants to receive Communion at Mass. So before the ceremony started, he explained carefully and emphatically that the unity of prayer was perfect, but that they were not ready for intercommunion. His congregation,

however, did not quite agree. "What happened," the celebrant recalled later, "was that the whole congregation spontaneously rose
as one man to come forward."

This is an experience of the discovery of community. "The whole
congregation spontaneously rose as one man." They were united.
No canon law united them. The building didn't unite them. Ties
of familiarity and long-standing friendship didn't unite them. They
were united in their desire to share the Lord's Supper. They discovered, right there in the dramatic action of the ritual, that they
were, in fact, united.

One could cite many other examples of communities coming
about spontaneously or — in cases where the community was
planned and organized — instances where community feeling came
about almost as naturally and smoothly as shifting gears in a car.
A deft speaker can unite an audience so that they react to him
"as one man," involved in the common tide of emotion. Before
the founding of the first labor unions, workers often "found" themselves united, in feeling and commitment and in a set of values and
beliefs. Today's black power groups are built on a common unity,
often that of frustration. The United Nations grew from a feeling
of community among nations. And many people have had the experience of developing a close, intimate circle of friends who, in the
beginning, found that they were often together before they thought

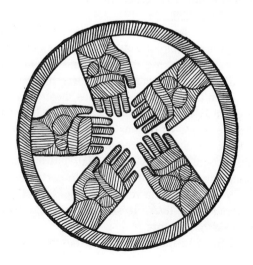

much about it. The creation of human communities such as these is vital to the Spirit's work of re-creating mankind.

Christ had promised the Spirit to his followers: "I will pray the Father and he will give you another counselor, to be with you forever . . . you know him for he dwells with you, and will be in you."

On Pentecost the Spirit Was Given to Them

"On the day of the Pentecost, they were all meeting together, when suddenly there came from the sky a sound like a violent blast of wind, and it filled the whole house where they were sitting. And they saw tongues like flames separating and settling one on each of them, and they were all filled with the Holy Spirit and began to say in foreign languages whatever the Spirit prompted them to utter."

Peter, who assumed leadership of the small group of Jews believing in Jesus, addressed the Jewish multitude gathered from all parts of the known world.

Peter's message was that Jesus was risen from the dead, that he was the Holy One of God, the fulfillment of the prophecies. He said that Jesus had taken his place at God's right hand as the Lord and had sent down the Spirit, the sign and gift of the messianic age.

Because Jesus rose from the dead, Peter said, people could no longer look at life as they had before. Because Jesus had risen from the dead, the world was different.

The Church became a flourishing community, with a brotherhood of life based on the leadership of Peter, the teaching of the apostles, communal prayer, the breaking of bread, and common property. Though it was still tied to Judaism and still worshipped in the temple, it was unique. In the group of Christians, Peter was not merely a teacher like other Jewish rabbis. He was the leader of the community. Unlike the Jews, Christians were no longer in search of the Messiah. After the Spirit descended on Peter and the others, they more fully recognized Jesus as Messiah and more deeply understood his meaning for their lives. Most importantly, they now expected that Christ would soon return to them in final glory. This expectation colored their lives. It strongly affected their understanding of the Jewish Scripture.

The prayer of the Christian community differed, too, from the prayer of the Jews. The Christians praised God for having raised Jesus from the dead. They prayed for Christ's quick return to them, and for strength in their faith until he would come.

The Christian breaking of the bread was different from the Jewish meal blessings. It was (1) a looking back to the paschal meal Jesus had eaten with the Twelve in the upper room; (2) a prayer for Jesus to be present among them then; and (3) a plea for Jesus to come and make all things new.

The custom of holding property in common grew up originally among Christians who believed that Jesus would soon come in glory. So it was unimportant for anyone to make any more money. In fact, no one would even need anything for himself. Yet they continued to hold property as a group for the sake of the poor among them.

The Unity and the Love, the Truth and the Life

What is the Holy Spirit's role in the creation of Christian community in today's world? How should Catholics view the Christian groups to which they belong?

The Catholic Church as a community, the neighborhood social action team, the religious order, the scientific research group, the volunteer workers in state hospitals, the family, and all kinds of human groups extend the Holy Spirit's work of bringing mankind to the fullness of Christ. The unity and love, the truth, life and growth discovered within the group are the signs of that Spirit.

We may understand the life of the Christian community better by discussing how various Catholics think about the Church as a community of believers. Consider three understandings of Christian community: (1) as a small town parish; (2) as the Body of Christ; (3) as the People of God. Each of these images help different Catholics understand the Church as a community but no one of them fully explains the Church. This is because the life of the Church is the work of God and remains a mystery.

In the *small town parish* (not the big city parish where few people know one another), there is often a feeling of belonging. Everyone knows everyone else. The priest is only a telephone call away, and is often a personal friend. It is just as easy to keep up with parish activities and attitudes as with anything else in the area. A broad mutual agreement of belief, attitudes, and feelings is not hard to maintain. The same people who worship side by side in church also often work closely together. They have attended the same schools; they know the same people. Community is experienced on many levels.

But the small town parish cannot usually be an adequate image or symbol of the Church. A small town will reflect a much narrower range of views, than, say, a city, a state, or a nation. Faith may be rigid, and people may find it difficult to grasp the way others with totally different worlds of experience and value believe in Christ. Neighborhood groups, too, inadvertently seal themselves off: Friends and strangers are identified and classified. In-group feelings separate people from the outside, and there is a definite "we" as opposed to "they." It is often hard to break into the circle of acquaintances in such a parish group.

Few Catholics in the United States today belong to country parishes where everyone knows everyone else. When they attend Mass on Sunday, most Catholics feel little or no "community" with those around them. So they must use different images for thinking about their experience of Christian community. Two such images are the Body of Christ and the People of God.

If a Catholic chooses to think of the Church as the *Body of Christ*, his perspective widens. A body is organic and alive and on the move. It is not limited to one place. It has vitality, personality, and mobility and is constantly developing. Because it can grow, it can look toward the future. And in the process, it can normally repair and heal itself. Such an idea of the Church is not mechanical. Developments happen naturally. Just as a body has a variety of functions and interacting members, the community has the capacity for sharing, for openness to growth and evolution.

But even this image of the Church leaves something to be desired. For one thing, there is the way it has been developed theologically — with opposition between head and body. The implication is that all the thinking, innovation, imagination, and decision-making come from the head, and that freedom and personal initiative are not the concern of the members. A second problem is that it may allow membership in the Christian community to be interpreted too narrowly. Furthermore, since the Holy Spirit is usually described as the "soul" of the body of Christ, it becomes difficult to explain his relationship to the people who are not members.

The documents of Vatican II emphasized another idea — the Church as the *People of God.* "I will write my Law in their hearts," says the prophet, "and I will be their God and they will be my people." This can be a very rich and illuminating image. For one thing, the idea conveys breadth. One is a member, not so much of a tiny neighborhood group, but of "a people," a new nation, a unity that could conceivably embrace the whole world. There is room for a great variety of relationships within this People, on its borders, and even outside it. The concept of authority is not removed but rather elevated and broadened into a more human context — one with more room for interaction, change, and improvement. According to this image, there is more room for hope, development, progress, and dedication to common goals.

One problem with the People of God image is that it makes demands on the Christian. Membership in a new people suggests that demands can be made on the individual either for the sake of the group or the more needy members of the group. For many, this may be unwelcome or downright unpalatable. The old clubby feeling is gone. The image doesn't stress the old idea of individual, personal relationship with God.

The People of God is a model with the scope needed for openminded thinking about the Christian message and mystery in the world. Perhaps the Church, acting as the People of God and considering itself as such, can make a greater contribution than ever before to the world and its full human development.

Discussion

1) Can you think of any cases where a sense of community has grown up among a group of people: for example, friendships with neighbors, groups of fellow students in college, friendships developed in PTA or political work, summer social action projects, Peace Corps volunteers, bowling teams, or movie clubs? Have you ever been involved in building such a community?

2) Can we say that there are ways in which such groups help to bring about the new creation? Or does this seem a rather inflated way of talking about very ordinary things? The theology of hope implies that nothing can be completely ordinary for a Christian who believes that Christ has already begun to save the world. Yet Christians experience many things — washing dishes, waiting for a

bus, talking to the neighbors — as very ordinary. Are they missing something of the Christian life?

3) When you think of the Church as a Christian community, as a bond of fellowship and friendship, which of the three models of community in the chapter would you find most fitting?

The small parish? Have you ever lived in a small parish? Do you know anyone who has? How might this experience affect a person's idea of Christian community? Do you think that the relative closeness of most Protestant congregations has an important effect on a Protestant's view of Christianity? From what you know about Protestants, how would you describe this effect?

The Body of Christ? Could you think of ways in which people in large cities could achieve the same sense of community as in a small parish? Would this be worth doing, or do you think that the present Catholic setup is the most practical and effective? Do you feel at home in a big city parish? Would it make a difference to you if you knew all the people around you at Mass on Sunday? Can the Church become just a lifeless abstraction in the mind of a Catholic when he isn't acquainted with the other members of his Christian community? Or are there religious values more important to Catholics than a sense of community and belonging? If so, what are they?

The People of God? The Second Vatican Council constantly speaks of the Christian community as "the People of God." What important Christian values do you find in this description of the Church? What are its weaknesses? Does it answer any of the problems of the small parish or of the big city parish?

Discovery of the World

How Common Effort Becomes Community

Sometimes people try to become free or help others to become free — as in the Czech moves toward independence in 1968, the Hungarian revolt of 1956, or the successful attempt of African nations to become independent of colonial powers. Sometimes people freely take responsibility for their fellow men — as in the formation of the Peace Corps, the Vista Volunteers, or the 1963 Washington march for racial equality. Sometimes people try to understand mankind and the world — as in the work of the World Council of Churches or the ecumenical religious community at Taize in France. The Holy Spirit can enter into every dimension of life. Some people feel that the Spirit is at work today shaping new kinds of political communities among university students throughout the world.

Many would reject the idea that the Spirit was operating in the rash of student revolutions in the spring and summer of 1968, or that the rebellions of young people from Paris to Morningside Heights, from Berlin to Berkeley over the past few years represented a force for political good. But the first of these does show us something about how human communities take shape.

It is interesting, with that in mind, to go back to Berkeley and 1964 and look at a recent — some would say one-sided — account of that "revolution" and how one writer saw it. In the fall of 1964, the Berkeley administration instituted new rules governing campus political activity. The changes might have meant that the political activist movement on campus — quite alive at that time — would be choked off. Reaction on campus was immediate and intense. Fifteen thousand students created a strike that shut down the university. The movement was important not in its size, but in his type. It was something new and unusual in recent United States college life, and it *felt* different.

Some say it all began one day when three thousand students

surrounded a police car containing a young man arrested for manning an illegal civil-rights pamphlets-and-slogans table. For two days, from a microphone placed on top of the car, the students carried on among themselves, a "spontaneous, free, and unmoderated public dialogue." The open microphone was the means of bringing into the open many of the issues and themes of what was called the Free Speech Movement.

During the hours of this police car protest and open microphone dialogue the students worked among themselves forming groups to collect food, arrange for pickets and sit-ins, and deal with the appearance of police. And the students began to discover that a new kind of political community was being born.

Michael Rossman, writing in *The Center Magazine* in May, 1968, recalled that the police car episode had ended in unresolved tension. When six hundred police massed on campus to "rescue" the car, the threat of violence affected the demonstrators but did not move them. They had spent six years coming away empty handed from lesser conflicts with the university administration. For these disillusioned and basically idealistic activists, the car was their first tangible "possession." Gathering around its odd altar was the first evidence they had that they were at last a community.

But the students didn't clash with the police in the end. Moved by the wish to avoid violence to the newly discovered community, representatives signed an agreement to call off the demonstration. They considered the existence of the community more important than success in resolving the formal conflicts that brought the community into being.

The mass activities of the next months gave other clues about the nature of the community. It had a distinctive style of working which gave shape to the vast output of energy among the students. Observers, impressed by the movement's power and efficiency, assumed that it was highly-organized and centralized, led by skilled and experienced individuals. On-campus observers say that it was in fact decentralized and disorganized, semi-leaderless, and run largely by novices. In most cases, people would recognize a need, then would experiment to find ways to fill that need — collecting bail money, correcting press distortions, providing a place where food could be prepared and signs stored, for example. People chose to work, and chose the work they would do; orders from on high and central discipline were unnatural. In this setting, a thousand people focused their energies into the movement.

Many people regretted that the community chose not to engage in political relations with the larger society. They knew that such a choice reflected a growing inability to find any meaning in committees, resolutions, and the like. What they often did not know was that the community of activists committed itself to a political existence fundamentally different from that of the parent society.

Some people described the student political action as a "form of theatre" — a staged event, something created specifically as food for newspaper reporters and television cameras.

Other people called the protest demonstrations "therapeutic." Students generally pass through a change of life at this time — facing marriage, military service, scholastic failure and the task of making personally important decisions. Protest marches were a good outlet for these pressures.

Still others labeled the movements at Berkeley as "defiant," "savage," "a setting for dope and sex." Many were less than happy with the number of non-students — both at Berkeley, and later at Columbia — who were involved in the rebellion. But despite the reluctance of the school administration to recognize the new political community, despite police intervention, despite the sense of powerlessness, of hopelessness and psychological strain that the youthful protesters felt from time to time, the community continued to exist.

Whether one agrees or disagrees with the purposes of the "student revolutions," accounts of them can serve to describe how communities "happen" around a certain sharing of purpose.

Understanding the Spirit Community

Among Christians today — as among the earliest Christians — there is no single understanding of the work of the Spirit. The early Christians felt that the Spirit Jesus had promised them was guiding and strengthening them while they waited for Christ's second coming. The biblical writers tried to explain the presence and help of Christ's Spirit in several other ways. Luke and the Acts of the Apostles, the fourth Gospel, and the writings of St. Paul show three related ways of understanding the role of the Spirit in the Church.

1) Luke and Acts were probably written between 80 and 90 A.D. almost 60 years after Christ's ascension. As a result the author was

not preoccupied with the immediate return of Christ, as, according
to Paul's earlier letters, was the first generation of Christians. Luke
realized that the Church would go on living just as the people of
Israel had done before Christ, but with a vital difference. Christ
had come and inaugurated a new era. Luke and Acts divide history
into three segments: the time before Christ, Christ's own life, and
the life of the Church until the Lord's return. According to Luke, the
Church received a mission during this final segment of history: "But
you shall receive power when the Holy Spirit has come upon you;
and you shall be my witnesses in Jerusalem and in all Judea and
Samaria and to the ends of the earth." Then Luke tells the story
of Pentecost. When the Holy Spirit first came upon the Church and
began to strengthen the disciples so that they were no longer afraid,
they then began to preach and heal in Christ's name. Luke's understanding of the work of the Spirit looks forward into the future
and sees the continuing history and witness of the Church being carried out with the help of the Spirit.

2) The Gospel of John was probably written between 90 and
100 A.D. Thus the author faced the same problem as did Luke:
How was Christ still present to his followers when he had not returned as soon as they expected? Though John's answer resembles
Luke's, it concentrates more on the effects of the Spirit in the lives
of individual Christians. Christians have experienced rebirth. They
are those who believe in Christ's name and have become children of
God. Through this rebirth in faith, they have communion with
God — a fellowship with the Father and the Son. With Luke, John
sees the Church as bearing witness to Christ both in its worship and
work. The Church is the community of believers to whom the world,
in its darkness, stands opposed.

While Luke said nothing about the nature of the Spirit, John
holds that the Spirit is God, and affirms the love of God to men. This
Spirit, or Comforter, convinces men of the things of God and re-
inforces them in their belief. Thus a union with Christ is real here and
now even though Christ has not yet returned. The Spirit reassures
men that he will come, and he also unites them with himself in the
present. Christians are united by the Spirit in a fellowship of love,
and in this union of love through the Spirit, people can relate
to each other and have communion with Christ.

3) The apostle Paul wrote much earlier than Luke or John, prob-

ably between the years 35 and 55 A.D. His understanding of the role and work of the Spirit was rich and complex. It is important to notice that nowhere do Paul's writings get very explicit about the relationship of the Spirit to God or Christ. Instead, he speaks of the Spirit of Jesus Christ, of Christ, of God's Son, of God, and of the living God, without much distinction.

According to Paul, the divine power which was manifest in Christ is present in the Church as the gift of the Spirit, both at Pentecost and later. This gift of the Spirit comes from heaven and is granted to all believers as adopted sons of God. The Spirit is the divine pledge of immortality. Christians now enjoy the life of grace, and this will be perfected by the resurrection of a spiritual body after death.

Furthermore, the indwelling of the Spirit in Christians brings about their sanctification here and now. The new life is known in Christ and sustained by the Spirit. It is shown by the increasing perfection of love among Christians, who form a brotherhood in the Body of Christ. The Spirit brings to various Christians gifts which are to be used for the building up of the Church. The Body of Christ constitutes a new spiritual order, a new community, replacing the Jewish people. Membership in the Body depends on the influence of the Spirit, who gives faith. The Church is a society which, though it allows for diversity, is unified in the Spirit. According to Paul, the Church is a sign and a witness to God's glory. Paul does not attempt to explain the nature of the Holy Spirit; he just points out that the Spirit "energizes" and "vitalizes" the Church.

Wasn't it at Pentecost that the Church was founded?

Biblical scholars have made it apparent that the writers of the New Testament were not writing a history in the modern sense. They were writing a document — or rather documents — that expressed for the believer the significance of what happened in Jesus' life, death, and resurrection.

Surely the account of Pentecost given in Acts makes abundantly clear that whatever we say about Jesus Christ founding the Church, we cannot mean that he founded it in the way Henry Ford began the Ford Motor Company. For if he had, Pentecost would have been unnecessary. Christ founded the Church, but its inauguration occurred when the Father — and Christ — sent the Holy Spirit (whom Paul called the Spirit of Christ).

The evangelists were concerned with demonstrating that there was some kind of continuity between Jesus' life on earth and the Church which came after him. However, the continuity or connection is not at all the same as the connection between a corporation and its dead founder. The reason is simple: Christ is alive and is acting in his Church in the power of his Spirit; and the Spirit is continually founding the Church, his people.

This explanation of Christ's founding the Church places great emphasis on the Church's present-day experience on the Spirit's activity within her, without giving up the past history of that experience.

Where Is the Spirit?

What are some of the characteristics of the Spirit's work in the Christian community in our own day? What are his purposes and how do we recognize them? How is his work related to the work of Jesus?

The Spirit is God as he is closest to us, as he comes to man in an inward way, in an enlightening, strengthening, unifying way. The Spirit's work is everything that helps the human community blossom into the fullness of love of Jesus Christ. The Spirit is present wherever people work together to form a genuine community, wherever they weld bonds of peace and friendship among individuals and nations on ever deeper levels. Wherever people try to overcome their lack of scientific knowledge or technical skills or their lack of understanding of one another, the Spirit is there. He is present wherever people try to live creatively human lives — in homes, offices, corporations, schools, in political and social life, in industry, religion, science, and the arts.

The Church as a community of persons, as a living, breathing, growing organism, manifests the presence of the Spirit. The Spirit's presence in the Church is characterized by its life, its dynamism, its renewal, and its continuity. Life is recognized wherever creative things happen and people are free to be themselves. Dynamism is the power that keeps mankind moving, thinking, maturing, producing. Renewal is what enables organizations and structures to think young again. Renewal happens, the prophet Ezekiel says, when dry bones are clothed with flesh and have new life breathed into them It is structures that allow, encourage, and strengthen human living

Continuity keeps mankind together, connects people with the past and moves them toward a future — in intellect, art, science, human relations.

The Spirit is the source of *unity* among men. The Spirit is at work when people recognize the dignity and value of their fellow man, when they open themselves to demanding relationships, when they are aware of being a part of things — part of America, a family, a church, a company, mankind. It is the unity which is a gift of the Spirit that moves Catholics and Protestants to sit down and talk together, that urges Christians to dialogue with Marxists and Communists.

The Spirit is the source of *truth*. In the Church, the biblical sense of fidelity is one way to understand truth. It means being *in* the truth, not just possessing the truth, as though it were a bright idea. God's fidelity to his people is the source of the Christian community's fidelity to him. The Spirit is at work creating fidelity in Christians; he will continue making it possible for them to be faithful.

The Spirit is also the source of truth in the sense of knowledge and understanding. He is at work helping men understand what is going on in the world, in society, and in their personal lives. The Spirit helps people discover, recognize, and even create meaning and value in their own lives, the life of the community, and in all of creation. Above all, the Spirit of truth helps people understand that God is here and now really redeeming mankind.

The Christian community recognizes that the Spirit acts everywhere in the world, not merely in the village Church and its members. The Church's purpose is to offer people specific ways to participate in God's work in the world.

There are many examples of the work of the Spirit in the creation of communities outside the Catholic Church, and still more outside the strictly religious sphere. Communities of Jews, for example, meet in underground synagogues behind the Iron Curtain. In their secret meetings, they demonstrate the effect of the Spirit in creating another kind of life within the suffocatingly oppressive atmosphere they feel around them. Throughout the world the Spirit is assembling people of many different religions to discuss unity and mutual understanding, to demand that men and nations recognize poverty and oppression and strive to end racial discrimination and war. Parents struggle to solve problems arising in their marriage — financial worries, the petty squabbles that can lead to separation or divorce, the how, when, and where of educating sons and daughters. These struggles are all signs of the Spirit at work.

Parents meet with teachers to discuss school administration and teaching techniques. People in a community take time to meet and welcome new neighbors, or to mobilize community thought and action toward open-housing laws. Again, the Spirit is evident.

Scientists hold meetings and establish international societies to share the results of their research. They express concern that the forces of nature which they unlock be channelled into peaceful uses, that their technological advances go toward human development and not human destruction.

The Spirit is at work in government and politics, helping statesmen to shape laws that promote justice, helping them to understand the needs and desires of citizens. The Spirit is at work in the law office, the police precinct office, the advertising office, the tenement, the classroom, and the United Nations assembly hall. The effects of the Spirit in these communities is a striking contrast to the places where guerilla warfare is a way of life, or areas where graft, bribery, and extortion are the rule, or organizations where the individual is never treated as a person in his job, his recreation, or in his neighborhood.

The Christian people are mediators for one another and for mankind; they convey God's gift of life, because the whole people is incorporated into Christ *the* mediator. It is the Spirit of the one mediator uniting men to the Father that is in them as the source of all good and humanizing work.

What is the relationship between the activity of the Spirit within the visible Church and outside the visible Church?

This question reduces to the frequently expressed one: What good is being a Catholic if God will save all men who are open to his grace in the world?

God is acting in the lives of all men, from the most primitive tree-worshipper to the holiest Christian. Considering that Christianity has not touched a large portion of the world's population, some Catholic theologians have begun to talk about Christianity as the "extraordinary" way to salvation and other ways to God as "ordinary."

The Christian believes that the acceptance of Christ as Lord is a proclamation of what God intends for all men. But while all men are living in the era of the Good News of Christ, many do not recognize this. It is the mission of the visible Church to be a sign to the world. By its preaching and sacraments it points to Christ as Lord and to his work as Good News for us.

Since God is calling men to the fullness of humanity through his Son, it is important that men be aware of their involvement in his effort of their fuller humanity. That effort involves man's participation in *God's* design for the world.

So, while the Spirit is acting outside of the visible Church, he also acts within the Church to urge the People of God to be a genuine and persuasive sign of what God desires for man.

Does the Spirit inspire practical activity or only doctrines to be believed?

We don't have to go back to St. Paul's letters to see the practical side of the Spirit's activity. Pope John XXIII often told how the idea of convoking an ecumenical council came to him in a flash. It brought with it a joy and peace that made it seem an inspiration of the Holy Spirit. And so an ecumenical council of far-reaching significance was set in motion.

But it is not only popes and saints who are inspired by the Holy Spirit. The Spirit is everywhere at work. For example, a Christian married couple can be confident that the Spirit will be concerned with their mutual love and growth in Christ.

Yet Christians who are concerned for the protection of helpless nations, like Christians who think the United States is waging a terribly destructive war, may be convinced that they *must* speak out, or else be unfaithful to the Holy Spirit. Christ's Spirit does not always speak in all people in one and the same way.

Is the Spirit the source of differences in the Church?

We know that the kind of unity that Paul saw did not exclude frank meetings between churchmen on basic issues. In Jerusalem Paul met Peter head-on in the dispute about the role of Jewish law and custom in the new community. This confrontation was a sharp one, but it would be wrong to suggest that the Holy Spirit was not active in it. It is extremely difficult to recognize the Spirit's work in individual events and activity. In the case of Paul and Peter, there were probably many Christians at the time who, while they took sides, were nevertheless shocked at the sharp encounter between two of their leaders. Yet in the perspective of history it is clear that the confrontation had to come if the basic identity of Christianity over against Judaism was to be established.

The way to truth is a zig-zag path. The Spirit is involved in the differences, sharp or mild, between members of the community as they clash. The kind of disunity that excludes the Spirit is a disunity that springs from pride, in a sense of exclusive possession of truth, or in envy, ambition, or hatred. To the extent that differences in the Church can bring out the truth of the Gospel, the Spirit is actively involved in these differences.

How can an individual decide what the Holy Spirit is asking him to do?

The ways in which a Christian can try to understand what the Holy Spirit is asking him to do are not hidden and secret. One's talents and deficiencies, his educational background, his physical make-up, all aspects of his daily experience can be avenues by which the Spirit leads him.

Discussion

1) Discuss other places besides the Catholic Church in which you feel the Spirit is at work: in political life, in world government, in business, in education, in family life, in social life, among young people. Or do you see few if any signs of the Spirit in these things? Discuss the expression "recognizing the action of the Spirit." How might the Spirit be working in the areas of art, science, technology, politics, human relations? Why might the Spirit urge Catholics to dialogue with non-Catholics, and even to dialogue with Marxists and Communists?

2) What does "rebirth in the Spirit" mean? What do baptism and confirmation mean in the light of the idea of rebirth in the Spirit? Is the idea of community as bond of fellowship important in understanding these sacraments?

3) Discuss the meaning of the term "the life of grace." People understand grace in many different ways. Some see it as a gift, some as new life, some as sanctifying power, some as bringing about a special relationship to God. Do you find these different images of grace confusing, or can you see in each of them some different insight into the mystery of grace? Do you prefer any one explanation of grace to the others?

4) If the Spirit is working in the modern world, he must be working towards the greater complexity and richness of human relationships, since greater and greater social complexity is the hallmark of our times. But why should the Spirit operate in this way? Greater complexity seems to produce greater anxieties, whole new ways of suffering and failing. Shouldn't the Spirit encourage greater simplicity in human activity and in relationships with others, for in that way he would encourage a deeper sense of being human and of concern for others? Isn't the encouragement of secular progress the very antithesis of a concern for people?

5) Today marriage and family patterns are changing. Wives can hold jobs, pursue professions, and make friends in areas completely separated from those she shares with her husband and children. Isn't this just the sort of complexity that detracts from truly human relationships, from the obligations of love and assistance she owes to her family? Shouldn't the Spirit be acting against the kind of world that permits such movement away from total involvement with her family? Or are there values in this situation which make for greater humanization?

Community
and
Institution

chapter 4

The Institution Emerges

Capturing the Spirit

The story of a group of people with an idea and the initiative to translate it into a going enterprise is almost as old as history itself. We saw it in the age of chivalry, the Renaissance, the Reformation, the drafting of the American constitution, the French Revolution. We see it today in our modern American labor unions, the American Red Cross, the World Bank, Goodwill Industries, Alcoholics Anonymous, the Congress for Racial Equality, the United Nations. All of these began with a small group of people who shared a dream, a need, and a conviction. To preserve this shared experience, communicate it to others, and give it life and growth, it was necessary for them to organize. This enabled them to maintain order and unity of purpose, to safeguard the values and original spirit and integrity of an idea, and to operate efficiently and productively in a world of "organizations."

There are hundreds of other examples close to home. Suppose a neighborhood community decides it needs a swimming pool. Neighborhood leaders organize a committee to collect money, find a suitable site, and arrange for architects and builders. Once the pool is built, membership fees must be set up and rules and regulations established. Married graduate students organize a baby-sitting pool

with schedules and meeting places. A group of civic-minded citizens organizes a program of "meals on wheels for the bedridden." A property-owners' group concerned about zoning ordinances and the appearance of their neighborhood is organized. People who share values, concerns, and goals find themselves thrown together to shape their particular social group.

Men are obliged to live at once in many contradictory worlds — spiritual, emotional, social, intellectual. But through all of these worlds runs a common thread that often binds men together. A group of U.S. servicemen stationed in Korea a few years back discovered that they all had a deep mutual interest in retail sales and merchandising. In the course of talking over their individual hopes for the future, they saw that their various ideas tended to come together. They decided to consolidate their resources. When they got out of service they organized a department store. One of the men became business manager, another sales manager, another the buyer, and so on.

Their dream — a very practical and this-worldly one — took root, and soon they were on their way. They opened a second store, then a third, a fourth, a fifth. Before long, this germ of an idea that originated in the remote, hostile battlefields of Korea had blossomed into a huge merchandising empire stretching all across the United States.

A group of enterprising dairy farmers was looking for a new market for their milk products. Discovering a common need and purpose, they formed a cooperative dairy. Gradually it got bigger and bigger. Today many of those original dairy farmers are on the board of directors of a multi-million dollar cooperative, complete with its own fleet of trucks and deliverymen.

If you took a stroll through Harlem, you would come across a new co-op supermarket owned by 300 Negroes and operated by Negro management. It arose out of an urgent community need to combat price-gouging by unscrupulous shop-owners. To launch their co-op, the Negro group managed to raise hundreds of thousands of dollars from sources both inside and outside the community. Now a thriving enterprise, the cooperative is forcing other stores in the area into more realistic, competitive pricing.

These are rather clear-cut examples, but often the final shape of the "dream" looks quite unlike the original one. What continues to unite these groups is the confidence that their institution can some-how keep and improve on the original dream. This is essential be-cause when the dream disappears, the most valuable motive is gone.

When a community transforms an objective into some kind of organization, there are both values and problems to be considered. Men dream dreams, not institutions. But institutions inevitably emerge to help make dreams real.

Awaiting the Promise

The first generation of Christians lived in the expectation that Christ's final coming would be "soon." They celebrated his pres-ence among them — and even more, his promise to come in glory — in their common meal. They prayed unceasingly, gather-ing in the temple and in their homes, breaking bread, sharing all they had with their fellow Christians and the poor. Some even left their homes and gathered on hilltops in excited anticipation of the coming judgment of the world and the return of the Lord.

But the Lord didn't return soon, as they had expected. He hasn't returned yet, and the Christian community continues to live on. In fact, the Christian Church has seen a lot of water flow under the bridge — and sadly, a lot of blood flow into the water. When the Lord didn't come as the first Christians expected, they realized that they had to think about a whole new approach to faith, for themselves and for those who knew the Christian faith only through association with Christians. They came to see that the Christ-faith was not an exclusive gift belonging to them alone as the last men in history, but a vision and a hope that belonged to all men of today and tomorrow.

So the community of Christians began to build for an earthly future. The Gospel of Christ spread beyond Israel to Syria and Egypt, and to Rome itself and its colonies. Out of the simplicity of that early Christian "community," lines of responsibility and au-thority began to emerge more clearly. As certain needs were con-stant, so were certain offices of service. Helpers and deacons were chosen for each local group of Christians; widows and the poor were provided for; missionaries were sent out. But as Christianity spread its shoots to the far corners of the Old World, it became harder to maintain unity of purpose and fidelity to the Gospel. In this period, heresy and schism were a constant threat. The exact meaning of Christ's message was debated, and the disputes often gave off far more heat than light.

Later on, leading disciples, such as Paul and Peter, found themselves in disagreement over the Christian "Way," and how it related to the Jewish dietary regulations, to circumcision, and to co-existence with pagans. Among the rank-and-file of the Christian community, differences seemed to be even more confusing and disheartening. Some abused the common meal; others refused to share their wealth with poorer Christians at home or with young struggling Christian communities in other countries. Their sense of Christ's nearness — and of his promise — began to recede.

The early Christians had to find ways to share their faith, vision, and hope with others. Instructions in faith had to be prepared; procedures for celebrating the eucharist had to be agreed upon; attitudes toward Jews and gentiles had to be decided.

They had to organize. They collected the sayings of Jesus. They developed organizations to care for the poor and the persecuted. They formulated rules for choosing Church officials. Customs for the community's life of prayer sprang up. Methods of dealing with reactionaries and with the unfaithful took shape.

Provision had to be made to preserve the Christian message. Expansion forward into history had to match the expansion outward into other lands — already in process.

How would new followers of the "Way" be instructed? Essentials of the Christian faith had to be made available for succeeding generations. Preaching and oral instruction were dominant; but missionaries, like Paul, wrote or dictated doctrinal and moral instruction to their communities. Sometimes these letters were circulated to other churches to be read aloud during the assembly.

Religious schools were established, and each had its own style of instruction. The style and method of teaching usually depended upon whom the schools were designed to serve. Christ had taught some simple fishermen and laborers in Israel; his message had to be relayed and made meaningful to people in Greece, Rome, Asia, Africa — people of differing education and experience. The well-educated, order-conscious Romans who adopted Christianity, for instance, were not comfortable in the vivid, poetic Hebrew writings because they were not Jews. Nor had they been steeped from childhood in the rich imagery of Old Testament promise.

Thus Christians built up institutions that would enable them to establish ground rules for communication, examine conflicting positions and problems, interact as a group, and make decisions affecting many people at once. And through the centuries, the institutions have helped preserve and transmit the values, meanings, and experiences of the first Christian community.

In the Context of Institution

What are some advantages and disadvantages of the Church as institution? Does history encourage us to be hopeful about the institutional Church?

Just as the institution of marriage gives a social and visible expression to the love of a man and a woman, so the formal institutions of Christianity should make it easier for people to see and share in the promise offered to the first followers of Christ. Paul even described the Church as the bride of Christ.

Because of its institutions, the Christian community is recognized as a sharer in the history of mankind. The Christian community exists within history, is contained by it, learns from it, reflects it, and indeed grows out of it. Therefore, the institutional structures of the Christian community can make it possible for the contemporary American to share in the experience and hope of the Church throughout the centuries.

The institution can make of the living Christian community a community of shared experience as well as of hope.

Christian tradition and the Church link our complex technological society with the simple, agrarian world in which Christ lived and taught — not by making them culturally similar, but by giving the later age a direction toward growth. Christ's own teaching and the experience of the early Christian community provide touchstones for interpreting the chaotic events of man's history, giving them meaning and coherence. Through them, men of many differing cultures can seek common understanding, not only of major historical events that affect us all, but of problems of individual life that often cut much deeper.

This is our faith and our way of life. But it is not without its hazards, for both the teachings of Christ and the institutional structure built to preserve those teachings are subject to misinterpretation, since they depend on fallible men to interpret and carry them out.

Because the Christian Church has had a long history and a great deal of experience, it is often able to strengthen and guide people in time of crisis. This does not mean that the Church as an institution has always succeeded in its efforts to understand and to meet the needs of a particular period.

Nevertheless, the Church has been a vital element in the process of history. It has responded to needs, created new structures, and fought the evil that was part of man's condition. It has been strong in establishing schools, especially during the centuries when a new Europe was rising — like a golden phoenix — out of the char and ashes of the Roman Empire. It has been strong in structuring new social and political systems. For example, when Roman Europe gave way to nation-states, the Church began her own reformation. The Church has shown concern in social problems. During the modern industrial revolution, the Church was busy — through workers, priests, bishops and even popes — trying to develop a Christian social ethic. Now, after Vatican II, the Church is struggling with a gigantic educational venture, trying to rebuild its institutional structure and bring attitudes in line with the inspiration of the Spirit: Channels of communication are multiplying between the various "orders" of the Church — bishops, priests, religious, and lay people. Modernization or adaptation in liturgy and eucharistic celebration is encouraged to achieve a new depth of Christian fellowship. Concern for the poor has at last been awakened in most sectors of the Christian community. Doctrines of the Church are being rethought in contemporary terms. A new attitude of acceptance is growing toward separated Christian brothers as well as toward non-Christians.

The Christian who has hope sees all these things as signs of the promise that God is working through the Church to achieve the full humanization of all mankind.

Discussion

1) Most of us either work in a highly structured and institutionalized organization or have some experience with such organizations (e.g., government agencies). Do you feel that the organization of the Church, with its Roman Curia, diocesan chancery offices, pope, bishops, and other functionaries, is similar to a large business or government agency? Does the Church's structure have the same

advantages and drawbacks as any large secular organization with highly organized and centralized management structures? Do most of the problems in the Church come from its organization, structure, and officialdom?

2) In the Gospels, Christ never seems concerned with founding a formally organized and highly structured institution. How then can the Church justify its present high degree of organization? Can you think of situations in the lives of Christians today in which it might be better to have a less highly organized and centralized Church structure?

3) What role does Catholic education play in the structure of the Church? Has its role changed since you were growing up? Is a parochial school system necessary to the proper functioning of the institution? What do you think of the criticism that Catholics have put too much emphasis on "official" Catholic education and not enough on Catholic education which has a deeper religious meaning in the world of today? When you were in parochial school or when you attended religious instruction classes, did you feel that you were being indoctrinated? Did you feel that little attempt was made there to teach you what the doctrines really meant?

4) In your experience, how have Catholic institutions such as the following nourished (or failed to nourish) the Christian spirit in your community: Confraternity of Christian Doctrine programs? Catholic Charities? parish societies such as Holy Name Society, Rosary/Altar Society, Mothers' Club? CYO? Money raising techniques such as collections, bingo, raffles, spiritual bouquet cards, dances, bazaars?

5) What are some of the institutions and customs of the Church which you have seen change in your own lifetime? What reasons were there for the changes? Should some of them have been changed earlier? Are there others that still need change? Are there new institutions which need to be created so that more effective dialogue can be carried on with non-Catholics, lapsed Catholics, ex-priests and ex-nuns?

6) What do you feel is the proper relationship between pastor and people in a parish? Do you feel that the people have any business involving themselves in questions of church finances and decisions concerning construction of new buildings and the scheduling of new organizations and programs?

In general, is it clear to you what role bishops, priests, religious brothers, and sisters play in the Church today? How do you see your role in the Church in comparison to theirs? Do you think it is a good idea for laymen to form close friendships with priests and religious?

Why is there more discipline and structure in the Catholic Church than in Protestant churches?

Models in History

A Church of Sheep

The new 1966 revised edition of the Baltimore catechism is hung up on sheep. Fully nineteen of its sixty-odd illustrations offer to urban, industrialized America the thought that Catholics are sheep. There is a picture of sheep streaming past a rough-hewn cross on which a lamb is hanging, dripping blood straight down onto their heads. As they pass the cross they wander into the background where a stream of heavenly water is pouring out of a cloud. In the sky a giant figure, with a long white beard and triangular halo, has

released a dove which seems to be flying toward the sheep hanging on the cross. The caption reads: "The Blood of Jesus cleanses and strengthens His sheep to follow Him to heaven." In another picture, a handful of sheep stand dumbly isolated in a small, rather cheerless corral, on whose walls are printed in capital letters, "One, Holy, Catholic, Apostolic." A robed, haloed, figure with shepherd's staff stands outside the gate. Several rather forlorn looking sheep wander around outside, some of them looking up at the figure. The caption reads: "The Church is the Sheepfold of Christ."

Among other interesting samples of the book's "art" is the picture of a small herd of sheep marching past a cross. Christ is suspended by one arm from the cross; blood drips from his side and from both his pierced hands. A lamb is wrapped around the crossbar over his head; blood dribbles from the lamb as well. As each of the sheep passes the cross, Christ leans down to touch it. The sheep then march off into a glorious light. The picture is entitled: "Jesus cleanses His sheep so that they will not have a single spot on them." Not only do sheep appear nineteen times in the text. People themselves in other pictures maintain a sheeplike appearance. They seem gentle, meek, totally passive, waiting for the herdsman. From this catechism one would have no idea that people can write books, build bridges, and fall in love.

Apart from the exaggeration of these images, the modern Christian has real difficulty accepting them as an image of mankind. Domestic sheep are stupid, dirty, and easily panicked. They have to be taken care of constantly. They have to be led to water and food, protected from harm, and kept from wild animals.

The images of God and of Christ as shepherds are powerful biblical images precisely because a good shepherd shows care and concern for his sheep. And the image was apt for Christ because his Palestine, was, after all, "sheep country." However, the use of the sheep model reaches the point of absurdity when the Christian's whole relationship to God, Christ, and his Church is pictured solely in its terms. This suggests that members of the Church are nothing more than a flock of identical-looking beasts of the field, all enjoying the same stupidity, helplessness and dumb, blind faith. In the catechism text, this model's application to the sacrament of marriage is interesting: "Matrimony is an action of Christ, the Good Shepherd. It is an action by which He unites two of His sheep, a man and a woman, in marriage, so that they can bring forth new members for His flock."

A Church for the Universe

Members of the Christian community have looked at their Church in many ways. Some imagined it as a sheepfold, and others saw it as a kind of clock ticking members toward eternity, while still others saw it as a ship at sea.

To really understand the Church, we must understand Paul. In his earlier letters he uses the term *ecclesia* (Church) for (1) the local congregations of believers in various towns, or (2) as title of affection for the oldest communities in Judea.

Later in his life, however, "the Church" takes on a more universal meaning for Paul. It becomes a crucial part of the "mystery of Christ." The Church is the one body in which all men are reconciled to God; in it the barrier between Jew and Greek is broken down. Paul sees Christ as head of the Church, which is his body, and therefore as head of all creation.

The unity of the Christian community in the Church is one of Paul's favorite insights. This unity results from the single purpose of the divine plan of salvation: "one Lord, one faith, one baptism."

Some of the models of the Church which Paul uses are "the Israel of God," "the Jerusalem above," "the temple of the living God," "the bride of Christ," "the body of Christ." He also speaks often of the Christian's duty to "build up" the Church as if it were a tower or a temple.

Christian Community Institutionalized

How should a Catholic look at the Church today? How should he view his place in the community of Christians? How should he respond to the institutional structures, the church regulations, clergy, bishops and the pope? What does his way of thinking about the Church have to do with the whole quality of his life?

Catholics have many different ways of picturing the Church and explaining its elements. They may have seen it as St. Peter's Basilica, as their local parish, or the people in the parish they know. Theologians develop similar "models" for understanding it and expressing the keen tension Christians feel between their sense of Christian community and their response to the Church's institutional structure.

Each Catholic, in fact, shapes and refines a model of the Church that satisfies his own understanding. In trying to grasp and illuminate the meaning and importance of other models of the Church and in trying to fit new facts and experiences into his own understanding, the Catholic is continually reshaping his image of the Church.

Catholics, experiencing a tension between the spirit and life of the personal Christian community which they share and the social and political structures of the institutional Church to which they belong, have found ways of picturing the Church and explaining its elements. In the sheepfold model, for example, grace is "food," faith is "following," and so on. These models reflect the personal background, education, temperament and experience of those who frame them. Each model has distinctive advantages and drawbacks. The sheepfold model, for instance, underlines dependency on God but does not help at all to explain Christian freedom and responsibility; it expresses, though somewhat distortedly, a sense of unity among Christians but says nothing about spontaneity, creativity, or individuality within the Church.

Models for a Pluralistic World

In the following pages, three among many different models of the Church are presented with a view toward stimulating the formation of models for the 1970's: the structure model, the history model, the renewal model. Each implies a certain understanding of (1) the universe, (2) Christ, (3) membership in the Church, (4) grace, (5) the Church as institution.

The Structure Model

Universe: In this model, the universe is thought of as a huge cosmic machine. Each of the parts was created by God and set in motion. Each element of the system has its proper function, its proper place in the system, its proper time of appearance in history. Since God created and governs the system in its every detail, he knows exactly where the universe is going. Most persons who use this model of the Church seem to feel that mankind and the world are going nowhere. At present, individuals are born and die, enter the great maw of the system and then pass out of it. At one point in the future, God will call a halt to the world and there will be no births or deaths. People will be with or without God for eternity.

Christ: In this model, Christ is seen as primarily an old-fashioned king and judge — high above the earth, beyond all the human hierarchy of pope and bishops, above Mary even, sitting at the right hand of God. He came to earth to set things right, when men refused to accept their proper function in the cosmic system. He gave mankind clear rules and moral regulations to guide the operation and entrusted the continual government of mankind to the leaders of his Church.

For the Christian in this model of the Church, faith is almost identical with obedience. Those who refuse to obey, to "fit" into the system, are punished by disapproval, by excommunication, and finally, by a denial of salvation — damnation.

Membership: Each person has a place where he belongs. Some call it a vocation. Each is supposed to find his pigeonhole in life and be saved within it. Each Catholic must find and accept his humble "place" or "state in life" or "status" within the institution. A few chosen ones find a vocation to celibacy, which gives them higher status. A very few make it to the top, as bishops. One man per generation gets to be pope.

Grace: From the Church the Catholic learns who he is and how he is to behave; to the Church he returns his willing obedience. Sin means trying to move out from one's proper place in the system or straying away from the proper path, but grace is the power to return to one's place and one's path and remain there. Grace enables a Catholic to fulfill his position in the Church and the universe.

Institution: According to this model, the institution is far-sighted enough to see that every person has his place, knows how to behave, and is helped to do so. Christ reinstituted order in the world through the institutional Church and dispenses grace (divine life) through this institutional ordering.

Values: This structure model — the sheepfold model is a variant of it — stresses docility and obedience as primary qualities of the Christian. The teaching and governing roles of the papacy and episcopate are emphasized. For some, this model includes the idea that Christ has virtually handed over his earthly shepherd's role to the hierarchy.

Since the world is all wound up and running on schedule, however, there is little creative initiative in terms of future developments open even to Church leaders. The task is simply to refuel and keep the ship on course, keep the train on the tracks. There is only a necessary minimum of social concern or involvement in the world, and very little hope for the world, if any.

The History Model

Universe: The history model is not concerned with describing the universe as a clock, a machine, or a system. The universe cannot be captured in a single concept. The universe is primarily the lived history of man in which God's creative and redemptive activity is at work. In the context of this model, the universe is for man. Man is the key to the world and its history. God created the world in terms of man. What is good for man is good for the world, and what is good for the world is good for man. Things in the world here and now are both good and bad; but God is working through men in history to overcome evil and suffering, toward the re-creation of mankind. As history moves into the future, no one can be sure of what God will be doing. Thus no one can know how God will accomplish the full humanity of man.

Christ: Within this model, Christ is not merely a figure of speech or an example of human moral perfection. He is primarily Lord of history. Christ is God who, risen from death, lives. He is Lord in power — including the power to re-create mankind. He has sent his Spirit to work out the fullness of the humanity of man. In this model, Jesus' resurrection is of supreme importance, because it points toward the event in human history which shows, once and for all, the involvement of God's power in the events of history.

Members: In this model, membership in the institutional Church is not crucial for the working out of God's project for man's future. All men are motivated by God's Spirit. The Spirit acts in the members of the Christian community, but not only, nor even chiefly, in the Church as institution.

Individual members of the Church are people who use theological tools to think. But they also use all the other tools — for example, the social and physical sciences, history, literature and personal experience. These members find themselves insisting that theology must learn from what is really going on.

Grace: Grace in this model is God's power to re-create mankind in the Spirit of Jesus Christ — the development of man to the measure of Christ's perfect and adult humanity.

Institution: This model soft pedals the institutional Church, while affirming the existence of a Christian and Catholic community whose purpose is to build up responsible human persons. The function of this community is to present the Christian Gospel clearly and intelligently. In this view of the Church, the institution can help insure that Christ's message will continue to be heard in the world, but the Church as an institutional apparatus has no claim to pre-eminence.

Values: The history model stresses responsibility for the Christian in the world and deep concern for all mankind. In many ways, it sees the growth and maturity of mankind as the final result of the process of Christ's re-creation of the world. This model does not offer the individual any mapped-out plan of life. It does not define or even govern behavior. In many ways, the Christian in this model is left quite alone. The world must be open to the Christian Gospel. The institutional Church may, if healthy, help to focus attention on the historical presence of Christ. But it is the life of Christ's Spirit, not the institution, that is of primary importance.

The Renewal Model

Universe: The renewal model sees the universe as evolving in some manner — perhaps biologically, perhaps spiritually, perhaps both. Hence the universe is not a cosmic machine. On the other hand, the historical meaning of the universe is already revealed; but questions remain about the final meaning of the unity of mankind. Thus the renewal model is not as "wide open" as the history model. Still, it is not indifferent to the world. It sees world history as salvation history. It sees the growing consciousness and unity of man as tied in with the increase in systems of organizations; the one cannot grow and develop without the other.

Christ: Christ, too, is seen from an evolutionary viewpoint. He is seen emphatically in two ways, as revealer and as founder of the Church. As revealer, he came historically to show us the Father and inaugurate the kingdom of God. But, alive and present to us today, he continually reveals to men meaning, value, purpose, and direction, and he invites mankind to work with him in achieving his "new creation." Second, the Christian in this model believes that Christ explicitly founded the Church and gave a sacred character to her teaching. Such a Christian might have difficulty with concrete doctrinal expressions of this teaching, but he believes that ultimately Christ's Spirit guarantees the Church's teaching an authority that no other organization or science possesses.

Members: Members adhere to the Church both as a community of believers and as an institution. Each member feels that he is intimately involved with the Body of Christ. This Body — no thanks to its members — offers him a guarantee of true meaning and value. For although the Church, especially today, is fragmented and filled with tension, Christ's Spirit resides somehow in this community. And so it is within this community that the Christian chooses to search for the resolution of his problems.

Grace: Grace in this model is the personal self-giving of God to men in God's creative, redemptive, and sanctifying activity among men. For the Christian in the renewal model, it is in and through the Church that the secret fact of the restoration of the world in Christ is revealed to man.

Institution: In the renewal model, the institution is evolving, too. In order to be of service to man, the institution adapts to the contemporary world view. The willingness to adapt explains why this is called the renewal model. In a sense, this is the Church as understood by Vatican II.

Renewal within the Church happens on two levels. On the surface, in the mechanics of things, there is a lot of trimming to do, tidying up of the shop. On a deeper level, there is a search for the root meaning and purpose of the institution and a constant concern for keeping true values alive and growing. Because the institution was originally founded by Christ, its doctrines are guaranteed to express God's revelation. As a matter of fact, the organized, teaching Church can be described as the "history of revelation as institutionalized."

Values: This model is open to hope. It expects that the promises of God, as well as the ways of mankind's fulfillment, will be made manifest in the Church, both as a community and as an institution. The Christian in this model is concerned for all mankind, but he approaches the world through the Church because he believes that the Church enjoys God's guarantee of true meaning and value.

The Church is seen also as a channel of service for mankind. But the Christian of the renewal model is apt to become preoccupied with details of surface renewal or the endless search for the true purpose of the Church, thus becoming so involved with the Church that he never looks beyond it to mankind.

MODELS OF THE CHURCH

STRUCTURE	HISTORY	RENEWAL

How the Universe is seen in each model of the Church:

God created a cosmic machine where each element has its proper place and function.	God created a universe in terms of man. Universe is lived history. God is working toward a future goal, defined only as the re-creation of mankind.	God created an evolving universe and revealed its meaning and future. World history is salvation history.

How Christ is seen in each model of the Church:

Christ is judge and ruler. He asks obedience from men. His objective is to set people on the right path, and punish those who refuse to "fit."	Christ is the Lord of history who is source of the trans-historical power which is working to humanize man.	Christ is revealer of God and his purposes, and founder of a Church to whose teaching he gave a sacred character.

How the Members are seen in each model of the Church:

Individuals find their identity according to the ordering of the universe, and become aware of themselves through finding their proper place in the institutional Church.	Individuals are motivated by the Spirit who acts in men, not necessarily in the institution. All who are involved in the humanization of man are participating in what God is doing.	Individual is searching for a solution to many life problems, but in belonging to the Church somehow feels he is a member of a sacral community, involved with the body of Christ which offers him a guarantee of meaning and value.

How Grace is seen in each model of the Church:

Jesus' power to bring each person to his proper place and path and keep him on the right track.	Jesus' power to recreate mankind being exercised among men by the Spirit of Jesus.	God's giving of himself to mankind in terms of creative, redemptive and sanctifying activity, exercised among men, revealed through the Church.

How Institution is seen in each model of the Church:

A hierarchically structured religious community which institutes order among Christians and dispenses grace through its members for the proper working of the system.	A community which presents the Christian message in a clear and intelligent fashion.	A continually self-renewing organism that adapts itself to contemporary man to better exercise its function as transmitter of God's revelation.

Discussion

1) Which models of the Church do you respond most favorably to? Do you wish the model you prefer would become more widely accepted in the Church? Do you find it upsetting that there are so many ways of thinking about the Church and Christ? How does your image of the Church now differ from the image you had of it as a child? Why did your image change?

2) If we collected together the different values which all the models emphasize, we would have a list which included the following: freedom of the individual conscience, spirit of obedience, respect for the hierarchy, concern for social action, openness to all men, personal concern and love for others. Is there any one model you could describe which contains all these values, or all the values which you would like to see operating in the Church?

3) One of the key themes of this chapter is the tension between the Church as a community and the Church as an institutional structure. Do you experience this tension at times? Do you know other people who do? Can this tension be overcome, or must the Christian learn to live with it as part of his Christian duty?

4) Have you ever personally experienced the Church as a community, as a felt bond of fellowship? Do the Mass, sermon, novenas,

missions and retreats help you feel this bond, or are they experienced as the same old things which you and the priest go through over and over again, acting just out of habit?

5) Do you know people who interpret the Church according to the structure model? Do they tend to be insecure or weak personalities? Are there also strong and self-possessed people who see the Church in this way? How would this model affect the daily life of a person who was inclined towards it? Would it tend to separate him from the world and from other people? What would the idea of Christian fellowship mean under this model? Does this model avoid the tension between community and institution? If it does avoid the tension, is the avoidance a good thing? What sort of people would be least attracted by the structure model? Are there ways of modifying it in order to make it more attractive to these people?

Are there elements in the Christian life which the structure model does not deal with; for example, freedom of conscience, involvement with human problems (politics, world hunger, the population explosion)?

6) Do you know Christians who think of the Church in terms of the history model? What kind of people are they: professional men, teachers, businessman, ordinary working people? How do the people who prefer the history model react to the idea of a hierarchy of pope, bishops, priests, religious? Are they people who would be likely to get involved in parish or civic activities? How would they look at such problems as the system of parochial schools, attendance at Sunday Mass, the role of the sacrament of penance in Christian life? Have you ever looked at the Church from the point of view of the history model? What are the attractive (and unattractive) points in looking at the Church in this way?

7) Can the renewal model be understood as a camouflage for either the structure model or the history model? If the renewal changes only external things, have any really important changes been made from the structure tradition? If the renewal changes fundamentals, haven't we admitted the history model's point that the Church institution isn't really very important, and may at times even be positively harmful to true Christianity?

What kinds of people do you think are attracted to the renewal model of the Church: creative people, artists, radicals, revolutionaries? Or housewives, office workers, family doctors, small businessmen? Or members of both groups? Would it surprise you to know that all these kinds of people were attracted to it? Why might they be attracted to it?

8) Probably no person can live the Christian life under one or another model exclusively. Is it possible for a person to live under each of them at different times? To form some combination of them? How would you describe the model of the Church under which you *do* live? Is it different from the model under which you think you *should* live? In what ways?

How do the models of the Church in your generation differ from those of your parents' generation? From those of your children's generation?

The Developing Institution

Phyllis McGinley, in the July 13, 1968 issue of *The Saturday Evening Post*, declared that the modern American family has evolved a new style of life. She feels they are more like frontier families than like their own parents. When Eastern or immigrant families moved out into the frontier, they left most moral and cultural absolutes behind them. They developed their own style of life, their own customs, their own ways of dealing with things.

Miss McGinley sees the new American family as being very similar. She feels that, contrary to all the "woe-sayers," this new kind of family is working out its own destiny and creating its own standards.

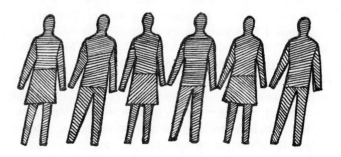

The typical young couple no longer lives comfortably secure in the shadow of parents and grandparents or among old friends and hallowed family memories. Rather, they tend to move away from their parents and to live by themselves in apartments. Indeed, young couples are willing to live almost anywhere rather than with their parents. The practice of large businesses, which constantly move their younger executives from city to city, accentuates this trend. At the same time there is a flexibility in the new young families: They are able to adapt themselves to different situations and locales with great ease; they look forward to moving frequently and traveling far in their lifetimes; they have to learn to take care of themselves and manage their lives, cope with their problems, alone. The scarcity of domestic help and the cost of unionized skilled workers forces young families to deal with household chores and repairs by themselves.

Prosperity has delivered this generation from the desperate poverty of the 1930's and has opened up a wide range of possible activities. Young people today throw themselves into business, politics, volunteer service, education, and the arts. Their disdain for security often amazes their parents.

They build their family structure around mutual commitment and aims rather than financial considerations. They devote themselves to understanding their children, to raising them for full and useful lives. In short, these families don't accept life as it is, presuming that it can't be changed; they try to create their future in as new a way as possible.

In these and many other respects the new American family finds itself returning to the freedom, initiative, creativity, mobility, flexibility, and closeness of pioneer American families. Miss McGinley says, "We are back where we began, on a frontier. That large, warm, papa-dominated Victorian family group is what we look back to wistfully, thinking it the norm. Actually it existed for less than half a century and then chiefly in fiction. . . .

"Families now resemble that vanished concept far less than they do the pioneer clusters at the start of our country's history. Like the pioneer families, they face a wilderness where few trails have been blazed, few signposts erected. Though the wilderness is moral and psychological rather than geographic, its dangers are real."

At the same time, Miss McGinley recognizes that a return to

the "frontier style of life" means the individual has vast personal responsibilities. "Under the impact of sociological pressures, pillars topple, established standards crumble. Religion, custom, common opinion — none is strong enough to regulate the new liberty. Ours is a bracing but a foreign climate. . . . As a consequence [the young people] have developed a remarkable self-sufficiency. I watch them walking their hardy paths and marvel at their stamina."

Wanted: A Superparent?

It is no easy thing to set out to conquer a new frontier. Thus it is not surprising that some, unsettled by this new situation, long for a "superparent" who might miraculously supply all the answers and solve all the problems. If somebody would just step up, tell us what to do, show us how to set things right, there'd be no need to worry so. We could just lean back and leave our worries to this Super Problem-Solver.

Frank Baum, in his delightful *Wizard of Oz*, has pictured just such a situation. Dorothy, a young Kansas girl, has been swept away in her home by a tornado. She arrives at the mysterious Land of Oz, a fairytale place where witches and wizards are real and her safe, secure Kansas seems terribly far away. She learns shortly after her arrival that the Wizard of Oz is probably the only one who can help her get home. She sets out to seek his aid. On the way she picks up some fellow-travelers: a Cowardly Lion who wants courage, a Tin Woodman who wants a heart, and a Scarecrow who wants a brain. Dorothy suggests that they accompany her to Oz: perhaps the Wizard will grant them their wishes.

When the pilgrims finally reach the Emerald City of Oz, however, they are rebuffed. The Wizard receives them in several grotesque shapes and says he will help them only if they dispose of the Wicked Witch of the West. They decide they will try, for there seems to be no other solution. They set out for the West and eventually succeed in destroying the Witch by melting her with a bucket of water. They returned to claim their reward from the Wizard. Finally, they got an appointment, for exactly 9:04 A.M. the next morning.

The four travelers passed a sleepless night, each thinking of the gift Oz had promised to bestow upon him.

Promptly at nine o'clock the next morning the green-whiskered soldier came to them and four minutes later they all went into the Throne Room of the Great Oz.

Of course each of them expected to see the Wizard in the shape he had taken before, and all were surprised when they looked about and saw no one at all in the room. They kept close to the door and closer to one another, for the stillness of the empty room was more dreadful than any of the forms they had seen Oz take.

Presently they heard a Voice, seeming to come from somewhere near the top of the great dome, and it said solemnly,

"I am Oz, the Great and Terrible. Why do you seek me?"

They looked again, in every part of the room, and then, seeing no one, Dorothy asked,

"Where are you?"

"I am everywhere," answered the Voice, "but to the eyes of common mortals I am invisible. I will now seat myself upon my throne, that you may converse with me." Indeed, the Voice seemed just then to come straight from the throne itself; so they walked toward it and stood in a row while Dorothy said:

"We have come to claim our promise, O, Oz."

"What promise?" asked Oz.

"You promised to send me back to Kansas when the Wicked Witch was destroyed," said the girl.

"You promised to give me brains," said the Scarecrow.

"And you promised to give me a heart," said the Tin Woodman.

"And you promised to give me courage," said the Cowardly Lion.

"Is the Wicked Witch really destroyed?" asked the Voice, and Dorothy thought it trembled a little.

"Yes," she answered, "I melted her with a bucket of water."

"Dear me," said the Voice; "how sudden! Well, come to me tomorrow, for I must have time to think it over."

"You've had plenty of time already," said the Tin Woodman angrily.

"We shan't wait a day longer," said the Scarecrow.

"You must keep your promises to us!" exclaimed Dorothy.

The Lion thought it might be as well to frighten the Wizard, so he gave a large, loud roar, which was so fierce and dreadful that Toto (Dorothy's little dog) jumped away from him in alarm and tipped over the screen that stood in a corner. As it fell with a crash, they looked that way; and the next moment all of them were filled with wonder. For they saw, standing in just the spot the screen had hidden, a little, old man, with a bald head and a wrinkled face, who seemed to be as much surprised as they were. The Tin Woodman, raising his axe, rushed toward the little man and cried out, "Who are you?"

"I am Oz, the Great and Terrible," said the little man, in a trembling voice, "but don't strike me — please don't! — and I'll do anything you want me to."

Our friends looked at him in surprise and dismay . . .

"No; you are all wrong," said the little man meekly. "I have been making believe."

"Making believe!" cried Dorothy. "Are you not a great Wizard?"

"Hush, my dear," he said; "don't speak so loud, or you will be overheard — and I should be ruined. I'm supposed to be a great Wizard."

"And aren't you?" she asked.

"Not a bit of it, my dear; I'm just a common man."

"You're more than that," said the Scarecrow, in a grieved tone; "you're a humbug."

"Exactly so!" declared the little man, rubbing his hands together as if it pleased him; "I am a humbug."

"But this is terrible," said the Tin Woodman; "how shall I ever get my heart?"

"Or I my courage?" asked the Lion.

"Or I my brains?" wailed the Scarecrow, wiping the tears from his eyes with his coat-sleeve . . .

"When you came to me, I was willing to promise anything if you would only do away with the . . . Witch; but, now that you have melted her I am ashamed to say that I cannot keep my promises. . . ."

"Can't you give me brains?" asked the Scarecrow.

"You don't need them. You are learning something every day . . . Experience is the only thing that brings knowledge, and the longer you are on earth the more experience you are sure to get."

"That may all be true," said the Scarecrow, "but I shall be very unhappy unless you give me brains."

"But how about my courage?" asked the Lion anxiously.

"You have plenty of courage, I am sure," answered Oz. "All you need is confidence in yourself. There is no living thing that is not afraid when it faces danger. True courage is in facing danger when you are afraid, and that kind of courage you have in plenty."

"Perhaps so, but I'm scared just the same," said the Lion . . .

"How about my heart?" asked the Tin Woodman.

"Why, as for that," answered Oz. "I think you are wrong to want a heart. If you only knew it, you are in luck not to have a heart."

"That must be a matter of opinion," said the Tin Woodman. "For my part, I will bear all the unhappiness without a murmur, if you will give me the heart."

And so the next day, when the four returned to see Oz, he tried to fulfill their wishes. He cut out a silk heart, stuffed it with sawdust and inserted it in the Tin Woodman's chest. He filled the Scarecrow's head with bran and placed pins and needles in it — to show how sharp he was. He gave the Lion a drink to make him courageous. But it is perfectly obvious that none of his "solutions" really worked. It was as he had said the previous day: They could have dealt with their problems on their own if they had only realized it. The wonderful Wizard of Oz, Great and Terrible, did not really have the magic key to all their problems. They worked their difficulties out themselves. And Dorothy's problem was solved by very practical means, not by "magic" from a "Wizard"; they made a balloon and escaped from Oz in it.

Baum's insight is that people have to look at their own situations and then try to solve them, that there are no magic, easy answers. Childish as his story is, it does point out the fact that solutions to problems and difficulties are far more likely to be worked out by men than to be mysteriously solved by a wizard or "superparent."

And in basic ways this is related to what Miss McGinley was saying about the modern American family. If Americans have become mobile, self-sufficient, and involved, then to long for the comfortable "answers" and "solutions" of yesterday is not really valuable. It is like wishing the Wizard of Oz would somehow make everything "all right." As problems and difficulties arise, people can only look at them seriously and try to deal with them. There is no point in wishing for some magical abacadabra that will make them go away.

This is just as true of the Church as it is of individuals and other organizations. To the new American family, finding its way as change sweeps over the world, the Church as a community and an institution needs to offer intelligent and imaginative responses. As the Wizard of Oz suggested, people often have far richer resources than they realize.

An Experiment in Community

One of the most imaginative and exciting responses in the American Catholic Church since Vatican II may be the Community of John XXIII, an experimental parish in Oklahoma City which has no property, boundaries, or restrictions on membership. Parish administration is handled by laymen. As its "spiritual administrator," Father William Nerin is a community employee rather than the man in charge. He receives a salary, lives in an apartment, and keeps regular office hours in a professional building. When invited, he attends the meeting of the administrative council. Father Nerin and lay members of the community address each other by first names. This adds to the sense of informality, joy, and even gaiety that, according to some reports, is the dominant mood of the organization.

The parish draws its members from Catholics who live in regular, established parishes, but remains open to anyone, anywhere, including non-Catholics. A Presbyterian minister attends Sunday sessions. A Baptist layman is on the board of directors. One of the leading members lists his formal religious affiliation as "Infidel." Members involve themselves individually in many public-service enterprises, particularly in civil rights and anti-poverty programs. As a group, the community has set up an Oklahoma branch of "The Fish," an organization dedicated to helping anyone anytime who is in any kind of need.

There is a three-hour limit on Sunday meetings, but excitment, interest and unabashed enthusiasm run so high that the limit is often not observed. The meetings themselves have been held in a rented room at Bishop McGuinness High School. In the liturgy, much is traditional, Father Nerin wears the standard vestments and continues to place the host on the receiver's tongue. Less traditional are the membership's jazzy little combo, the vibrant singing, the conscious sharing by children in the meaning of the community's liturgy. Also less traditional is the sense of community and common purpose, feeling, and expression.

Finding the Essentials

In all this talk of community and institution, in all the welter of change and renewal in the Church, how does a person know what the essentials are? How does he separate the gold from the dross? What is to be saved and carried on, and what is to be discarded and left behind?

The Christian community, the body of Christ, is the important thing. For the revelation and gift of God can be grasped and believed and brought to life only in the human experience. The institutions that comprise the formal organization of the Church are at the service of community. No individual institution has a right to destroy Christian community for its own survival.

A primary purpose of the Church is the development of a human community enriched with God's revelation and gift of life and love. The Church is to help persons connect and "make the scene": to relate and identify with one another in unity and truth, to make sense out of the world and feel at ease in it, to help resolve serious questions about life, suffering, and death. Its customs and practices, its expression and organization are supposed to provide meaning and value and to give direction and hope.

But there are times when things are overly institutionalized, and the institution must be overhauled or remodeled if it is not eventually to become dead and useless. The size and power of some organizations become stifling hindrances rather than aids to people in the delicate business of living out their lives. It is easy for institutions and structures to lose their flexibility, grace, and simplicity that typified their youth.

Attempts to legislate the spirit, and control God, can turn the Church into man's structure, not God's. If the Christian is to recognize the essentials of his faith and hope, he needs a sharp, discerning eye.

Institutions have power to hand on life; they also have the power to deprive a community of the depth experiences it needs to live, believe, hope, and grow.

The Christian community is a people of promise, a people looking to the future, constantly on the move. It is ever new and ever vital, yet ever a community. Because it is a community, its experience and hope must be expressed, externalized, formulated. Because it is a community ever new, its institutional forms are subject to the changes of history.

The growth and development of doctrine and the understanding of what the Christian life is all about today, and how it is to be lived, comes from everyone living the Christian life.

When the question arises, "What are the essentials of the Christian life today?" the traditionalist would say, "It is for the Church to decide," meaning the Church hierarchy, the pope, bishops, and pastors. Others would also say, "It is for the Church to decide," but for them the Church means the People of God, the entire Christian community. They are the Church. The Spirit is working in the Christian people, not merely in bishops and Catholic columnists. These others feel that the Spirit wants the whole Christian community to share in teaching, in helping one another find what the "essentials" are, in offering one another their knowledge and experience, in discussing today's problems and possibilities in the light of the Gospel of promise.

Vatican II has called Catholic Christians to honesty and openness in dialogue with one another, with pastors, priests and bishops. For all — laymen, priests, and bishops — *are* the People of God.

In the chapter on the People of God in the Constitution on the Church there is the following remarkable passage:

"The body of the faithful as a whole, anointed as they are by the Holy One, cannot err in matters of belief. Thanks to a supernatural sense of the faith which characterizes the people as a whole, it manifests this unerring quality when "from the bishops down to the last member of the laity," it shows universal agreement in matters of faith and morals.

"For, by this sense of faith which is aroused and sustained by the Spirit of truth, God's People accepts not the word of men but the very word of God. It clings without fail to the faith once delivered to the saints, penetrates it more deeply by accurate insights, and applies it more thoroughly to life. All this it does under the guidance of a sacred teaching authority to which it loyally defers."

We see priests disobeying their bishops and theologians disagreeing with the pope on important issues. They claim that the Holy Spirit is with *them*. Laymen, too, invoke the Spirit for pacifist dem-

onstrations and protests against their pastors. Who really is following the lead of the Holy Spirit in the contemporary church?

There isn't any easy test to resolve this question so simply.
When Catherine of Siena criticized the pope at Avignon, nobody was
thinking, "But she's a saint. She can do this sort of thing." The
pope must have felt that she was a menace and a threat, but finally
he came to believe that God's command was coming through this
woman's voice.

But it is not simply a question of holiness. Reflection is also
required. The decision whether the Holy Spirit is with a man who
seems to be speaking or acting "out of turn" is not simple. If the
situation is a complex one, the data has to be sifted and the insights
of Christian tradition applied.

For example, a man who insists that it is his Christian duty to
criticize America's Vietnam policy because it is motivated solely by
national selfishness can be judged only by one who makes the
effort to decide whether the charge is true or not.

In any such conflict of conscience, it would be better to sift out
the arguments and views expressed than to identify the Spirit as
being on one side or the other.

Discussion

1) "A primary purpose of the Church is the development of a
community of humans enriched with God's revelation and gift of
life and love." How does the Church achieve this purpose? Has it
always achieved this purpose? Can you think of any notable cases
where the Church has failed to achieve its purpose? (Are you thinking of the Church as the sum of all Christians or as an official
hierarchical structure?)

2) Consider some occasions when the teaching authority has at-
tempted to legislate in the field of personal morals: motion pictures,
women's clothing, reading matter, birth control, attendance at Mass,
fast and abstinence. Do you think that there is a place in the Church
for dissent from official positions in these matters?

3) If a person expressed interest in becoming a Catholic, what
do you think would be the most important thing to tell him about
the Church as fellowship and a community? About the Church as
an institution?

If a newly ordained priest assigned to your parish asked your advice on how he could best serve the parish, what would you tell him?

4) If a young person came to you and wanted to enter the priest-hood or the religious life, would you be inclined to encourage or discourage him? What would be the relationship between your advice to the person and your view of the Church as a community and as an institution? Would your advice change if this young person were your own son or daughter? Has your attitude toward religious vocations changed in the last ten years? Why?

5) Discuss ways in which the Church has changed in your life-time and predict ways in which it will change in your children's lifetime. What is your reaction to the rapidly accelerating rate of change in the Church today? Does the material in this chapter shed any light on the proper way of reacting to this rapid change? Do you think many other people see the Church the way you do?

Celebration
of
the Promise

chapter 5

Worship

A Common Meal

New Yorkers do not surprise easily. They like to consider themselves tough, practical, and shrewd in all the ways of the world. But one bright, sunny morning even New Yorkers were taken aback when 5,000 suburbanites from as far away as West Virginia converged on a dingy East Harlem slum area and joined local residents in a massive clean-up. Side by side, Negroes, Puerto Ricans, and whites cleaned out rat-infested cellars, painted everything within reach for a brush, repaired broken plumbing, replaced crumbling woodwork. As the hours sped by, this tiny corner of Harlem took on a rare new look of vividness and vitality. At noon the workers wiped away their common covering of sweat and grime and gathered at makeshift lunch tables in the middle of the street. Munching sandwiches, gulping ice-cold soft drinks and sharing jokes and banter, many discovered that something wonderful was happening — on both sides of the color and language barrier.

After the clean-up many cynics labelled the whole affair "tokenism," a feeble effort by whites to salve their collective conscience with a bucket of paint and a little elbow grease. That may have been true in some cases. But there was far more involved than that.

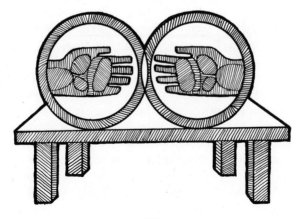

Monsignor Robert Fox, described by fellow New York priests as "charismatic" and "prophetic," was the man who spearheaded the project. What he wanted for the ghetto resident was to acquire a pride in his neighborhood and to "listen" to the voice of hope in the streets. In turn, he wanted suburbanites actually to see the plight of the slum-dweller. He wanted them to see what it was like to be a victim, and not a manipulator, of one's environment. He wanted the suburbanite to know how to relate to the people in the ghetto as persons.

Everyone who was there that day knew that clean streets and brightly-colored tenements would not solve the urban crisis. But it was at least a start toward bringing the two worlds together. And in the end, in fact, it did create a genuine spirit of fellowship that spanned the distance from White Plains to East Harlem and the even vaster psychological distance that separates America's haves and have-nots.

In many cases the feeling of that day in East Harlem still has not vanished, though the suburbanites themselves are long gone and the paint they applied is already dull and dirty. Something was born that day that could remain in that little pocket of misery for years. For many, the meal that whites, Negroes and Puerto Ricans took together that day satisfied more than bodily hunger.

In much the same way the recognition of some achievement gains much vaster dimension if a ceremony or other formal observance is involved. Would the Nobel Peace Prize be quite the same without the pomp and "ritual" of the Stockholm ceremony? Even university sit-ins can be a kind of ceremony of shared concern, calling attention to some lack of student dignity or freedom. Two friends who meet after a long separation stop by a favorite restaurant and enjoy a private little ceremonial dinner. It, too, is a symbolic ritual, with a sacredness and warmth all its own. A Resurrection City sprouts up in the nation's capital. Even though it fails to be the symbol its planners had hoped, it helps some people symbolically to share and celebrate their common dream. A college graduating class celebrates its imminent departure for the beckoning world outside; an alumni group from the same school gathers to toast those bygone collegiate days when its members were young and life was new and rich.

The same sense of sharing that finds expression in celebration marks religious life as well. When an adult or infant is baptized, the ceremony and the festivities that follow are communal celebrations. Family and friends welcome another human being into their shared life of faith and love, and the sharing is a cause for joy.

In marriage one's life is pledged to and shared with another. This stepping into another person's life is an entrance into community. The ordination of a priest is a celebration by the whole Christian community, because the community of believers is being given a man ordained for community service. And God is showing his power to raise up men who, in spite of their weakness, agree to be servants of the Christian mysteries and of Christians' hope.

At Mass all the people are celebrating, not just the priest. They are celebrating in the present, but also in remembrance and in anticipation of Christ's promise of life. When a man goes to church every Sunday, he realizes, even if he doesn't always think of it, that the priest facing him across the altar is doing something which the early Church recorded as being Christ's last will and testament. He is looking back. But he is also looking forward. He also realizes that the Mass is a ritual of hope, enacted "until he comes again." And he knows as well that the grace-giving event of that Sunday Mass is an expression of the presence of the risen Lord among his people.

Mass occurs these days in many forms: the solemn cadences of high Mass (now almost always sung in English), the normal Sunday dialogue Mass, the teenage folk Mass, the home liturgy in living and dining rooms. All these and others are forms which the Eucharist is taking in the Christian community. All these are shapes of the central worship of the modern-day Roman Catholic. But is a folk Mass or home liturgy really worship? Is a balloon-floating, castanets-and-bongos Mass really worthy to be presented to God as worship?

The Meaning of Worship

What is worship?

One way of looking at worship — in its broadest sense — is to say that worship is the praise given to God by men who are trying to share in what God is doing in the world and in their lives.

Often when people think of worship they think of certain gestures: genuflecting when entering a church, kneeling before a statue, bowing of the head, and so forth. Such gestures are meaningful to many people; but today's theologians, reflecting on the varied forms that worship has taken in the history of Christianity, distinguish between the visible, more outward shows of worship and the real, interior act of worshipping. Kneeling, for example, was not the earliest position of prayer — standing was. And it was only in feudal times when men knelt before their liege lord, that kneeling became a religious gesture for the European world. A Catholic writer like Leslie Dewart suggests that the gesture of kneeling in the presence of God may disappear now that man is "coming of age" in God's presence. His point is that the gesture may be rather empty of meaning, since almost no one kneels before earthly lords anymore.

Whether or not one agrees, Dewart's suggestion clarifies the question. Gestures are not necessarily real acts of worship. Neither are attendance at Mass and at benediction of the Blessed Sacrament, or the performance of all the other forms of public prayers and devotions — unless, of course, they include true reverence for God.

But there is a broader concept of worship which should be understood before any particular forms of private worship or of public, communal worship are discussed. The broad notion of worship stated above embraces all the ways in which men give praise to God, knowingly or unknowingly, publicly or privately. St. Irenaeus, an early Church Father, expresses succinctly his view of what the praise or "glory" of God really means: *gloria Dei homo vivens* — the glory of God is the living man: what glorifies God is authentic humanity. This means that the worship which God most desires is the life and commitment of a man who is alert as a Christian to what is going on in his world, who is sharing in it and contributing to it to the full extent of his talents. According to Irenaeus and the early Church, God is worshipped in the most fundamental way when men are responsive to his activity in the world and try to remain open to the persons they encounter, participating in the work of God, which is, after all, to increase the life of man.

The teenager rocking to the music of his favorite record, the accountant hard at work on April 10 to line up a hapless client's books, the child busy with his building blocks — all are, or can be, worshipping the Lord in some way. So, too, is the judge who tries to help delinquent boys brought before him, the college student who plans his career in terms of what he can do to help solve the poverty problem, or the salesclerk who takes a personal interest in his customer's request.

It is against this background or notion of worship that we can best appreciate what the more familiar gestures and words of worship are all about.

Take the Mass for Instance

For centuries the Mass has been viewed as the central act of worship of the Catholic community. The congregation participated in the eucharistic liturgy in its own fashion and the bishops were responsible for its structure and content. But there had been constant change and flexibility.

Then in the late Middle Ages the liturgy in the West became more and more fixed. In the sixteenth century the Protestant reformers so upset Catholic bishops and popes that the rite of Mass was legislated in every detail and became absolutely rigid in form. This had its advantages. For one thing, the unity of the Church was visible in the Latin Mass throughout the world. Catholics attending Mass could always be certain of what would go on (at least externally — not all Catholics knew very much about the Mass). The Latin language and the antiquity of the service allowed Catholics to share an experience that was universal in both space and time: The San Franciscan was not worshipping God alone, but with Parisians of the seventeenth *and* twentieth centuries. So even if many Catholics prayed the rosary or kept themselves busy with their own private devotions during Mass, they still felt involved in a mysterious and ancient ritual that went far beyond them in scope and meaning.

All that is changed now. Catholics are seeing, sometimes to their dismay, that the accent now seems to fall on variety, change, lay participation, new and less formal arrangements, and contemporary forms of music at Mass. Anyone who has joined in a home liturgy knows what a different view one gets when something as sacred as the Mass occurs in the most familiar of surroundings. He can't help thinking that this resembles the Eucharist that the early Christians celebrated, since there were few church buildings in the early centuries.

Home liturgies have now been allowed and encouraged by the bishops of many dioceses. But what is the Catholic to think about the so-called "underground churches"?

Some people are quite willing to consider "underground churches" as havens for "kooky" Catholics who feel that they can do anything they want to the liturgy, even in defiance of the proper authorities. Other Catholics, including a number of bishops, feel that the "underground churches" deserve to be taken seriously, even if they sometimes offend other people's tastes and judgment. The liturgy has a deeply pastoral significance, so that the need many feel for a radically new liturgy may be telling us something important about the future shape of Christian worship. After all, much of the Mass was invented by Christians through the centuries and was not part of Christ's institution at the last supper. What the members of "underground churches" are trying to say is that the liturgy belongs to the whole people of God to celebrate and adapt. According to this view, not just any kind of liturgical change will serve; it must be guided by at least two basic rules. The changes must: (1) show a solid understanding of the nature of religious ritual and history of the liturgy, and (2) respond to the genuine need that people now feel for a religious attitude and a set of practices that fit the times.

Mass in the Future

It is possible to see the Mass moving in several directions. If these directions are understood and appreciated, a great deal of anxiety regarding future changes can be averted; Catholics will be expecting them.

The first direction: community. The Eucharist, the Mass, is a celebration that belongs to the Christian community. This has two main implications: (1) the Mass is meant for people who have a sense of something-Christian-in-common; and (2) it strengthens and enlarges that sense. The degree of community feeling achieved before an individual Mass can, of course, vary and can be very small — as in many large urban parishes. But it can be argued that the kind of Christian communities called for in our pluralistic, non-Christian, mobile and anonymous society must be socially oriented. They must be closely intimate subgroups that are capable of moving out into and serving the larger community.

For example, a group of professional men and women meet in an apartment in a Chicago suburb once every few weeks to celebrate the Eucharist. At these meetings they also take time to talk about their involvement in community relations organizations, meditate on Scripture and report on their reading. Most of the men and women are professional people. Some of them see each other only at these meetings. Others work in the same office or on the same community projects. None of them look upon the liturgy as something reserved for an exclusive "in-group." They bring to the meetings a spirit of closeness to one another and a concern for others; and the discussion and celebration of the Eucharist with their chaplain develops and nourishes their Christian commitment. They try to leave each meeting with a new sense of responsibility for the world. Between meetings, when they go to Mass in their parishes, they carry with them a sense of what a community of people having-something-Christian-in-common can be like. The larger parish congregation reminds them of the fact that their lives and worship are part of something much broader than their small group. There is evidence that groups such as these may represent the direction that things will take in the future.

A second feature of the liturgy of the future may be its simplified character and its emphasis on the ordinariness of the elements involved. In the days when Catholic culture was dominant, large public church buildings were the ordinary places of worship, and the ceremonies tended to match the grandeur of the buildings. All this is necessary, some would say, if man is to maintain his sense of the sacred.

But the Christian sense of the sacred is tied to ordinary things. Christ's life is communicated to a Christian in the breaking of bread and drinking of the cup. Two more ordinary actions are hard to imagine. The mystery of faith lies in ordinary actions shared by Christians and not in any man-made wonder like an imposing church building that overpowers people with its grandeur. There are many advantages in impressive church architecture. But to some people, large church buildings suggest a gulf between ordinary life and Christian life; and in these turbulent days such a gulf is intolerable to many. If Christ is met in the eating and drinking of ordinary bread and wine, this basic fact says something important about Christianity: the availability to all of the extraordinary Christian reality. This may not be an entirely new realization for the Church. But it may have an altogether new impact on the Mass of the future. Ordinariness — along with a renewed sense of community — is the Eucharistic wave of the future.

Discussion

1) Do you experience Sunday Mass in your home parish as a celebration? Why or why not? If you were asked to offer suggestions for making the Mass more like a celebration, what changes would you make? Are you comfortable at Mass? Do you feel that you are a part of what is going on? Why do you think people fall asleep at Mass? Is Mass for them something boring, unenjoyable, unimportant?

2) The discussion seems to imply that painting a block in East Harlem, celebrating a homecoming, attending Mass, and receiving the sacraments have something in common. Do you have difficulty making the connection between these events? What reason could you give for your difficulty?

3) How do you react to underground Masses you have read about or heard about? Can you give specific reasons for liking or disliking them? Why do you think the people who go to them like them? Should experimentation with the eucharist liturgy be permitted to continue? Why or why not? Would you personally encourage it? Have you ever taken part in a "different" kind of liturgy? Do you think the church is the best place to celebrate Mass? Do you think it should be the only place for Mass?

4) Do you think that the ways of standing, sitting, and kneeling at Mass are an important and meaningful part of Christian worship? Should Catholics develop new rituals more suited to contemporary ideas about prayer and worship? Or should we abolish set rituals and gestures altogether?

5) Some Catholics prefer the fullest community participation at Mass, while others prefer the traditional silent Mass. Some prefer to listen to the choir sing, others would like everyone to sing. Can the preferences of these different people be satisfied? Can there be a compromise, or does it seem that inevitably there will be a multiplicity of forms of Mass? Does the idea of many Mass forms bother you?

Theology and Sacrament

Where Have All the Sacraments Gone?

How does contemporary theology view the sacraments?

Theology today views the sacraments as signs of what God has promised men and as a partial realization and sharing of those promises.

Down through the ages, theologians have described the sacraments in many different ways. In the 12th century Peter Lombard said a sacrament was "the visible form of invisible grace." He also called it "an outward and visible sign of an inward divine grace; the sign aptly represents the grace and actually imparts it to the recipient." Thomas Aquinas in the thirteenth century sometimes described a sacrament as "that whereby anything is made sacred." A contemporary theologian has said that, in the fullest sense of the word, a sacrament is "the pledge of Christ's availability to a particular individual." Another modern view defines a sacrament as "a sacred sign of worship by which we come into intimate personal contact with Christ and receive his graces . . . and by which we join with Christ especially in his great action of dying and rising." Then there is the definition of the Baltimore Catechism: "A sacrament is an outward sign instituted by Christ to give grace."

For all the variety of viewpoint, there is no suggestion here that one should single out one of these definitions and stick by it. In fact, the Church has not officially shown preference for any one particular description. If the reader looks closely at each, he will see that some of them emphasize the sacraments as means of grace; others emphasize a personal meeting or encounter with Christ. The last is a more recent theological emphasis; but it is intended to clarify the meaning of the expression, "means of grace," which has come to sound rather mechanical and even slightly magical.

Each of the sacraments is an intimate part of the life of the Christian community as a whole. This is so true that Catholic theologians today often tend to speak of the Church, the Christian community itself, as the "fundamental sacrament" — as *the* basic sign in which Christ, now risen and at the right hand of the Father, is present and active in the life of men. At particular moments in a person's life this sign branches out into more specific signs of meeting with Christ: initiation in baptism, strengthening in confirmation, reconciliation in penance, and so forth.

The main problem with speaking of the Church as *the* sign or *the* sacrament is that the concept tends to make the Church appear as some reality outside ourselves, independent of the community of individual Christians. The Church becomes a kind of holy atmosphere, an all-enveloping fluid which surrounds and sustains Christian people, but in the end is somehow distinct from the human beings who make up the People of God. However, Vatican II's Constitution on the Church strongly suggests that the idea of the Church as a reality different from the People is incorrect. The sacrament of Christ's presence and activity in the world is nothing else but the many men, women, and children who make that presence of Christ visible and active, and who celebrate it. The sacrament of the Church is all these people, not simply as a series of individuals, but in their unity. Their bond is the Spirit of Christ, the Holy Spirit. It is in them that the Church is "the sign raised among the nations."

Theologians like Edward Schillebeeckx seem to feel that the traditional seven sacraments can be properly understood only if they are viewed as among the concrete ways in which the Church, the one main sacrament, is effective in the lives of men.

This link between the individual sacraments and the one basic sacrament, the Church, implies that every sacrament involves the whole community of believers. Yet, it involves not only the community interrelationship but also a two-way movement from the praying Church to God and from God in response to the praying Church. The basic reason for this two-fold structure (which is not equally evident in each sacrament) is that the People of God are praying people, to whose prayers God has promised to respond. Thus each sacrament is liturgical. For liturgy occurs when the people pray as a people, and their prayer receives the response from God promised in and by Christ. This response takes the form of what Catholics call the sacrament.

In baptism, for example, the Church prays that the person will become a fully graced member of the Christian community, and the rite of baptism both symbolizes and produces God's active response to the Church's prayer. Again, in the Eucharist, the Church prays for the full unity of Christians with Christ; the sharing of the eucharistic meal symbolizes and brings about God's response to such a request. Future changes in the shape of the sacraments will be made according to these principles — community involvement and the two-fold movement of prayer. The changes thus highlight the community and liturgical dimensions of each sacrament.

People may be disturbed by changes in the way sacraments are administered because they feel that anything instituted by Christ must be unchangeable. And the official teaching authority of the Church declared at the Council of Trent that the seven sacraments were instituted by Christ. Do these changes then create a contradiction?

Theologians today are aware of what the Church's teaching authority has said in regard to Christ's instituting the sacraments; they are also equally aware that the scriptural accounts mention at most three sacraments: baptism, penance (the forgiveness of sin) and the Eucharist. In the Gospels, it is hard to trace the institution of the other four sacraments. The establishment of the Church, which occurred in the resurrection and ascension of Christ and the sending of the Spirit, is enough to guarantee that an official prayer for God's saving help, when uttered by the official Church, is a situation affecting the eternal welfare of a Christian and will be heard by God. This is a sacrament.

The Church, considered as the People of God, has a great deal to say regarding the way the sacraments will "look." In fact, some sacraments, such as penance and marriage, took centuries to acquire the shape and meaning they now have.

It is quite likely, for example, that early Christian marriages in the West closely followed the Roman pattern; the difference came when Christians substituted a eucharist celebration for the Roman offering to Jupiter. In the centuries following, other elements of the ceremony appeared. Ambrose mentioned the bridal veil, Isidore of Seville recorded the use of a ring, Gregory of Nazianzen also wrote of the bride and groom's joining their right hands. By the ninth century a two-part ritual for Christian marriage had developed, involving (1) delivery of a dowry and a legal document, followed at some later time by (2) a nuptial Mass and a solemn blessing of the couple, who often wore crowns as they left the church. The present day Christian marriage ceremony — the texts of the Mass and blessing — come from the Middle Ages. In its Constitution on the Sacred Liturgy, Vatican Council II encourages further revision and adaptation to contemporary conditions: "The marriage rite now found in the Roman Ritual is to be revised in such a way that the grace of the sacrament is more clearly signified and the responsibilities of the partners are taught." The Constitution underscores the fact that the Christian people play an important role in shaping the sacramental rite of marriage; it recommends retaining "other praiseworthy customs and ceremonies" if they are traditional in a certain area, and reminds regional authority that each region is "free to draw upon its own rite suited to the usages of place and people."

It is important to remember this development in understanding and ritual for each of the sacraments, especially when there is talk that general community confession, for example, may become commonplace and not restricted to emergency situations like the battlefield. There are difficult questions involved here. But what we regard as the shape of various sacraments is not the only shape they can assume. And pastoral considerations (how will the new shape affect and help the faith of the community?) are as important as historical and theological factors. Thus, if the increasing sense of community fostered by liturgical change in the Mass leads people to look toward the sacrament of penance for a similar sense of community, the liturgy of that sacrament may have to change as well.

Evolution in the shape of sacraments is an entirely natural process, if only because each of the sacraments is related to each of the others in the lives of contemporary Christians. Sometimes the ritual of one of the sacraments — even one as basic as the Eucharist — may change to some degree. And the change in ritual affects a person's experience of the sacrament.

For example, in recent years, Catholic practice has de-emphasized the Eucharist as a time to be alone with God and explained it in terms of a communal celebration. As people experience the importance of the Eucharist as a communal celebration, they look to the other sacraments to reflect this experience. It is not surprising, then, that some Catholics who have shared the experience of community at the Eucharist should show a growing interest in general, communal confession of sin and less interest in periodic private confession. This sort of experience underlines the close relationship of the sacraments, one to another, in the life of Christians.

Once the Christian understands the Church as the fundamental sacrament and appreciates the communal nature of sacraments, individual sacraments of the Church appear in a new light.

Baptism signals the entry of a person into the visible Church community; through the Church the person participates in the saving power of Christ's cross and resurrection.

Confirmation is a deepening and enrichment of the initiation into the life of the Church begun in baptism; here the young Christian's "coming of age" in the Church community is duly noted and fostered.

In the Eucharist the Christian meets not only Christ's saving action but also the personal presence of the risen Lord under the forms of bread and wine. This is the central sacrament of the Christian life: the table of fellowship and the perfect sacrifice of praise.

In the sacrament of the anointing of the sick, the Church joins the sick person to implore God's help in strengthening him in body and soul. The oil — used by athletes in antiquity — symbolizes the strength and vitality for which they pray.

Penance is the sacrament of reconciliation, in which the sinner becomes reconciled to God under the sign of becoming reconciled to the Church, the community of the faithful.

The other two sacraments designate special classes of persons for service in the Church. In this they differ from the others. In the sacrament of matrimony the secular reality of marriage is incorporated into the saving grace of Christ, and help is given by God to build a Christian communion between the partners and in the family. In the sacrament of orders men are ordained to the service of the community for celebrating the Eucharist, ministering the other sacraments and preaching God's word.

Should the times and places for the sacraments be legislated or should they be left flexible?

This question really concerns the future shape of the sacraments. Though it is true that the Church can legislate times and places, the issue more and more is how details about the sacraments can be legislated for the Christian community. Society is becoming so mobile and people are becoming so aware of each individual's development as a unique process that it is increasingly difficult for theologians to come up with suggestions that are universally applicable. Confirmation, for instance, seems to make more sense if it is administered when a person is really coming of age in the Church. And our expanding understanding of the Eucharist seems to encourage celebration by truly free Christians, Christians who are celebrating because they *want* to celebrate (which doesn't just mean being in a good mood). Even the question of infant baptism is being discussed: Some emphasize that the child is born into an objectively redeemed world, a world saved by Christ. They agree that to be born into a good Christian home could in itself be a form of initiation into the Church — an initiation which may be brought to a deeper level by baptism. But this initiation is not achieved solely by the reception of that sacrament as an infant. So they think baptism at a later age may now be more appropriate.

Thus the times and places of the administration of the sacraments demand serious discussion, not only by theologians and Church officials, but by all those involved in the sacramental life of the Church and those who want to take an intelligent part in the full Christian life.

In what way is the Eucharist the central sacrament in Christian life?

Perhaps the best way to answer this is to see how Christ instituted the Eucharist. At the last supper Jesus raised to a new level a religious custom that was familiar to the Jews. A formal Jewish meal was a meal full of blessings; the more solemn the meal, the more solemn and numerous the blessings. The blessing was the presence of Yahweh, a presence promised to his people by the prophets, not only at the end of time but in all they did in their daily lives here and now. Partaking of the food was a partaking of the blessing because the food was blessed and was, in a sense, itself the blessing. Thus when Jesus took the bread, gave thanks, and broke it, then took the wine, gave thanks, and gave it to them, saying, "This is my body; this is my blood," he was really saying: "Partake of the blessing which is God's presence, my presence, by partaking of the food, the bread and wine."

This "last will and testament" left to his disciples — the Eucharist — was Christ's way of continuing, all through the time of his absence, his fellowship at table with the men committed to him and with their followers as well. Death and resurrection might intervene, but his presence among them would remain; and they would recognize him in each other, in the breaking of the bread.

The Eucharist is the central act of the community because in it, by sharing in the body and blood of the Lord, men share in his passover from death to resurrection. Thus the Eucharist is the firmest sign of hope given to Christians, hope that the fellowship with Christ, which is not present as sign, will someday be theirs to enjoy fully.

Discussion

1) What is your reaction to the idea that Christ is the principal sacrament and the seven sacraments are revelations of Christ's basic sacramental reality? Does it make sense to you? Would you have difficulty explaining this idea of the sacraments to children? Do you think this book has abandoned the traditional theory of the sacraments?

2) Some theologians describe the sacraments as "encounters with Christ." Do you like this way of expressing the reality of the sacraments? Does it express anything in your own experience of the sacraments? Are there other ways of describing the sacraments which you find more attractive?

3) If the new understanding of sacraments were maintained, wouldn't baptism have to be postponed until adulthood? In the same context, at what age do you think that penance, Holy Eucharist, and confirmation would first be administered? Do you think a new understanding of these sacraments would change the ceremony of

the sacraments so much that we might not recognize them? Would you like that? What are your reasons? Are you satisfied with the sacraments exactly as they are now?

4) Do you find parts of the ceremony of the sacraments meaningless or boring? Take the actual texts of the marriage ceremony, of baptism, or of the ordination of a priest. Do you find the readings appropriate? Filled with joy and hope? Do you find the prayers repetitious? Are you comfortable with the language of the marriage ceremony? Does the baptismal rite of the marriage ceremony forget about the people in the congregation and merely concentrate on the individual(s) receiving the sacrament? Is this the way you feel it should be, or should all the people in attendance be made to feel themselves a part of the celebration? How would you change the ceremonies if you were given the opportunity? How could the sacraments be made more alive, more a part of contemporary Christian life?

Part III
THE STRUGGLE FOR UNDERSTANDING

Social
Challenge
and
Response

chapter 6

Crisis As Opportunity

The World As an Emergency Room

"Human beings," George Bernard Shaw once said, "are the only animals of which I am thoroughly and cravenly afraid." To find out why, one need only visit any big-city hospital emergency room.

A fourteen-year-old, unconscious from an overdose of heroin, is carried in by his buddies. For the third time this year, a young alcoholic is back again and trying to climb the walls. Nurses tie him to the bed. He keeps screaming that he's falling, that giant green monsters are trying to tear off his legs. Two policemen bring in a groaning, pulpy heap of flesh. This is what remains of an Ivy League graduate student who was flying high on LSD and decided that he was God; to prove it, he hurled himself in front of a crosstown bus. On the other side of the room is a junkie who died of some bad stuff before they could get the needle out of his arm. Over there is a pathetic hollow-eyed little girl crippled for life because her sadistic father beat her up for kicks. Near the wall is a derelict blind from wood alcohol sold by enterprising teenagers.

In the midst of the most profound social and technological revolution that history has ever witnessed, the pace of American progress reveals only how much further there is to go. Southeast Asia

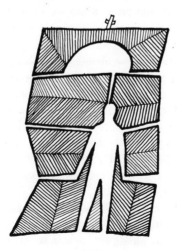

147

still reverberates to the fearful thunder of war. Disease, and poverty still stalk the malodorous streets of Harlem, and hospital emergency wards are still jammed with the victims of man's senseless inhumanity to man.

Suffocating Mixture

One author describes a New York City tenement: "The smells inside the tenement on 100th Street, Manhattan were a suffocating mixture of rotting food, rancid mattresses, dead rodents, dirt, and the stale odors of human life. . . ."

The State Commissioner of Public Health in New York is empowered to reserve hospital space for the treatment of addicts. This authority, however, has seldom been exercised. The reason, feels lawyer William Stringfellow, is the bad public image that it might receive if it became identified as a "tank" for drying out addicts. He writes:

"Why expect more of the legislatures than this? It is not, mind you, that they are ignorant of the problem. . . . They all know the recommendations of those, many of them experts, who have been close to this issue. But expect no action from them. There is no great public interest and no significant political advantage accruing to legislative action in this field. Addicts aren't voters! . . . All the addicts have on their side is need."

Men live in a two-sided world, divided between mutually hostile black and white, rich and poor, those with many opportunities and those with none. There are tensions and divisions between nations, between generations, between factions.

In *Crisis in America: Hope through Action,* a group of Christians discuss the anguish and turmoil in today's tortured world and seek ways of responding creatively to the crisis. They write:

"The Chinese word for crisis contains two characters — one for change and one for opportunity. As profoundly committed Christians who see God at work in the world, we must believe that our own crisis carries the hope of a better world. We now know that while the new conditions have created a crisis, they have also provided the means of resolving it."

In "Machine, Promise or Threat?" Robert Hamill writes: "Jews and Christians have long been compassionate, but we've never until recently had in our hands the power to make our compassion effective. To heal the sick, to feed the hungry, are commands which now tell us to use the oxygen tent and artificial lung and drugs, and nutrition research, food processing, the deep freeze, etc. . . . For now we are able to do what we have long been commanded — namely, to relieve the misery of our fellow man."

Response and the Gospel

Does the idea of social justice hold an important place in the Christian life? Does the Bible talk about it much?

The Christian response to social need comes on two levels: (1) words and actions in response to human suffering, and (2) the different kinds of response.

First, in his concern for the needs of mankind, Jesus preached more than mere kindness and good works. He responded to human suffering with firm, meaningful actions. He cured the blind, the crippled, the madman, the leper. He dealt with Jew and Samaritan, Phoenician and Roman, rich and poor, virtuous and wicked.

He never separated his work of healing the spirit from that of healing the body. When crowds followed him for days without eating in order to hear him speak of the kingdom, it was he who remembered their bodily needs and fed them. "I have compassion on

the crowd," he said, "because they have been with me for three days, and have nothing to eat. I will not send them away hungry."

When John the Baptist sent his disciples to ask Jesus if he were "he who is to come," Jesus sent back proof in deeds as well as words: "Go and tell John what you have seen and heard; the blind receive their sight, the lame walk, lepers are cleansed, and the deaf hear, the dead are raised up, the poor have the good news preached to them." Jesus was a man of action. He demanded that all his followers spend themselves in order to heal human suffering, whether on the road to Jericho or on East 100th Street in New York City.

Second, Scripture recognizes several different kinds of response to human suffering. There is, for example, the response of personal charity, and the response of social justice.

Traditionally, many Christians believed that their main obligation to others lay in private charity for those who could not care for themselves. This took in the sick and the poor, the widowed and the orphaned. "But if anyone has the world's goods and sees his brother in need, yet closes his heart against him, how does God's love abide in him?"

As an example of private kindness and concern, Jesus tells the story of the man who was attacked and beaten by robbers on a trip from Jerusalem to Jericho. On the road that day, at least one man stood ready to help overcome both suffering and selfishness. He was the Good Samaritan, the man who felt compassion for a fellow being and went out of his way to help him. He treated the man's wounds, set him on his own beast, brought him to an inn, and took care of him.

The modern political life of man, however, calls for a different kind of response to social injustice. Social injustice cannot be overcome by simply multiplying individual acts of personal charity. Today most Christians recognize that they cannot merely be responsible to others as individuals. Responsibility lies on another dimension of human society as well. It lies on the level of social and political institutions, including public authority, businesses and corporations, social customs, law and order, welfare organizations, and so forth. These institutions must also be made truly human as the setting for human growth.

Actually this notion of responding to social injustice through social and political institutions is not as new as it might seem. The prophet Isaiah thundered against unjust rulers in the eighth century B.C. "Woe to those who enact unjust statutes and who write oppressive decrees, depriving the needy of judgment and robbing my people's poor of their rights, making widows their plunder, and orphans their prey."

Jesus also saw the necessity for social change. He lashed out at the scribes and Pharisees for using their positions to lead the people astray. They were "blind guides" for the people who trust in them as the guardians of true worship. They "shut the kingdom of heaven against men."

The scribes and Pharisees had not combined their authority with justice. They were the kind of men against whom the prophets spoke. Ideas of social justice have developed in the past few centuries, and today notions of justice place heavy responsibility upon those in power. Justice is built on a solid Christian tradition of concern that authority be a source of humanization, not suffering and dehumanization.

A Church for Men

The Church and Social Responsibility

In the past hundred years, the Church has come to recognize that Christ's command of charity applies to social classes and political groups as well as to individuals. In this response to human need the Church has affirmed its right to speak out against political, social, and economic injustice.

This affirmation has not always been easy. In 1891, after half a century of political and economic turmoil and oppression, Pope Leo XIII defended the rights of the working man in his encyclical *Rerum Novarum*. There were Catholics who thought that he was turning socialist. In 1961, when Pope John issued his encyclical *Mater et Magistra*, a number of American Catholic conservatives denounced his talk of "socialization" and wisecracked: "Mater, si, Magistra, no."

In the same way, Vatican Council II spoke out on controversial issues of social injustice, for world government, and for an end to the arms race: "It is our clear duty, then, to strain every muscle as we work for the time when all war can be completely outlawed by international consent. This goal undoubtedly requires the establishment of some universal public authority acknowledged as such by all, and endowed with effective power to safeguard, on the behalf of all, security, regard for justice, and respect for rights.

"But before this hoped for authority can be set up, the highest existing international centers must devote themselves vigorously to the pursuit of better means for obtaining common security. Peace must be born of mutual trust between nations rather than imposed on them through fear of one another's weapons. Hence everyone must labor to put an end at last to the arms race, and to make a true beginning of disarmament."

Many of the Church's recent social pronouncements have carried a distinctly liberal cast. But if the Church has not been afraid to offend conservatives in its teaching function, neither has it feared offense to liberals in reaffirming the Church's traditional condemnation of atheistic Communism as basically inhuman.

In his encyclical *The Development of Peoples* in 1967, Pope Paul VI spoke explicitly of the responsibility of the developed nations toward the underdeveloped:

"Although it is normal that a nation should be the first to benefit from the gifts that providence has bestowed on it as the fruit of the labours of its people, still no country can claim on that account to keep its wealth for itself alone. Every nation must produce more and better quality goods to give to all its inhabitants a truly human standard of living, and also contribute to the common development of the human race. Given the increasing needs of the underdeveloped countries, it should be considered quite normal for an advanced country to devote a part of its production to meet their needs, and to train teachers, engineers, technicians and scholars prepared to put their knowledge and their skill at the disposal of less fortunate peoples."

Here in the United States, the bishops faced the problem of racial discrimination and segregation that is corroding much of American life. The United States Commission on Civil Disorders (The Kerner Report) described American society as moving rapidly in two opposing directions, toward two societies "one black, one white: separate and unequal." The 1968 national statement of the American bishops is a direct response to the Commission's report:

"The Catholic Church, which comprises nearly one-quarter of American society, with institutions that deeply affect all phases of that society, can hardly consider itself immune to the criticism of this nation's racial attitudes. . . . There is no time for breast-beating. . . . There is no time for idle talk; positive action must be taken to heal this rift, to build solid bridges between white and black men and within the white and black communities themselves.

"The Church, because of its divine mission and the human institutions at its disposal, has within its power to be a major force in reshaping American society into a truly democratic society in which all men are true equals, in which their lives can truly reflect the fact that they are created in the image and likeness of God."

The document cuts right to the heart of the problem:

"The moral and doctrinal heresy called racism works through people and through institutions. The Church's efforts must be two-pronged: directed at both 'personal racism' — combating it in the minds and hearts of its largely white membership — and at 'institutional racism,' cleansing its institutions and organizational life. The question must be asked of each diocese, each parish, each Church agency or organization: 'Does every aspect of its work support truly open, Christian behavior, or does it tend to reinforce the walls of separation and of white superiority?' "

The bishops call for a mobilization of all effective means for bridging the gap between whites and blacks and between urban dwellers and suburbanites. The document prescribes united action in the areas of constitutional law, labor unions, interreligious cooperation, news media, education, family life, health programs, housing, and employment.

The statement winds up quoting the words of the Commission on Civil Disorders: There can be no higher priority for national action and no higher claim on the nation's conscience."

Social Concern

In the Gospels Christ shows — and demands — active, enlightened, and immediate concern for others in response to their needs. What is the connection between this social concern and Christ's purpose in becoming man?

Christ became man to accomplish the redemption of man. But the redemption of man as he is today is inseparable from the redemption of the political, social, and economic institutions which man builds for himself and which strongly influence his attitudes, values, and conduct. While these institutions reflect man's initiative and human creativity, they also reflect the evil and confusion of all human life. Christ is concerned with the institutions of human living. They too must be redeemed and re-created if man is to be made truly human.

This does not mean, however, that Christians are committed to any particular means of redeeming social, political, and economic life. And because of the Christian's recognition of the radical confusion and ambiguity of life, he should be wary of over-simplified ideas on social redemption. If there were some single human plan which could perfect man's true humanity, the power of God would not be necessary to bring it about. True Christian concern for other men does not include unthinking enthusiasm and impetuous acting. It requires careful consideration of what should be done and the best ways of doing it.

In other words, the Christian can never separate the need for reform from the need for repentance. A belief in reform is the belief that certain institutions in government, in economic life, and in the everyday relationships between men are less than human, and must therefore be changed. Repentance involves the recognition of man's limited abilities for good and seemingly endless capacity for evil. In this understanding of the term, repentance has nothing to do with feelings of sorrow for specific wrong acts. Repentance in a person is rather the constant recognition that men can't do the job alone, that it is God's power and not man's which will ultimately bring salvation. "Without me you can do nothing."

The Christian is also called upon to remember that it is God's power — not his — that ultimately brings the end of evil.

The Christian is called upon to remember his obligation to others, since he is and will be judged in the light of this obligation. "I was hungry and you gave me to eat; I was thirsty and you gave me to drink; I was a stranger and you took me in; naked and you covered me; sick and you visited me; I was in prison and you came to me."

How does a Christian deal with particular social and political issues like the draft, U.S. involvement in Southeast Asia, or racial change? Is there one specific Christian attitude toward these issues?

There is no one Christian attitude on the complex political and social problems that face us today. Christians can only do the best that they can to make sense out of the situation in which they find themselves and try to develop ways of solving the problems at hand. Inevitably, different situations and temperaments produce different opinions among Christians, in some cases, very deep differences.

The radical reformer, for example, demands an immediate end to all political and social evils. The suffering that they produce is so great that any toleration of them makes a mockery of Christianity. He wants every improvement to be a reformation, an upheaval if necessary. Many Christians tend to be leery of the radical reformer's message. But it has strong biblical roots. Over and over again, the Old Testament prophets emphasized that there could never be any compromise with injustice. Amos directed some searing remarks to the "establishment" of his day, the wealthy and ruling classes, even the priests:

"Listen to this, you cows of Bashan, living in the mountains of Samaria, oppressing the needy, crushing the poor, saying to your husbands, 'Bring us something to drink!' . . . The days are coming when you will be dragged out with hooks, the very last of you with prongs . . . woe to those ensconced so snugly in Zion and to those who feel so safe on the mountains of Samaria, those famous men of this first of nations to whom the house of Israel goes as client . . . lying on ivory beds, and sprawling on their divans, they dine on lambs from the flock . . . they drink wine by the bowlful, and use the finest oil for anointing themselves, but about the ruin of Joseph (Israel) they do not care at all. . . . But let justice flow like water and integrity like an unfailing stream. . . ."

Many of Christ's teachings display an approach to problems that could hardly be described as "polite, careful conservatism." For example:

"If your right eye causes you to sin, pluck it out and throw it away; for it is better that a part of your body perish than your whole body be thrown into hell. And if your right hand makes you sin, cut it off and cast it from you; for it is better that a part of your body be lost than that your whole body should go into hell."

Prophets for the City of Man

The anti-war efforts of Fathers Daniel and Philip Berrigan demonstrate a radical interpretation of Christianity. These two brothers believe that compromise with the evil of the Vietnam war is impossible for a true Christian. Realizing their personal helplessness to stop the fighting, they decided to express their opposition symbolically. Late in 1967, Philip Berrigan entered a draft board office with a few friends and poured animal blood over draft records. The action was symbolic. But the penalty for defacing government records was concrete. Berrigan was tried, convicted, and sentenced to six years in jail. While out on bail he decided to offer another symbol of his resistance to the war. He and his brother, Daniel, stole some draft records and burned them, as another act of defiance against a system they vilified as "rotten and inhuman."

To many of the rising generation of Christian radicals, the Berrigans are an inspiration. They are spoken of as prophets and martyrs. To other Christians, however, the Berrigans are a scandal — arrogant, annoying, and embarrassing.

Calmer and more cautious Christians have their own way of responding to the social challenge. They recognize as do the radicals that we must work unceasingly to stamp out evil. But they believe that the world is far too complex and its problems far too subtle for radical righteousness to get us very far. Man is not God, nor is it for him to bring about the new creation. Man's sin can only be overcome by God. Human education and reform just aren't enough according to this group of Christians. They believe that those who overemphasize radical action are a new kind of Pharisee — they put their faith in their own power and righteousness, rather than in the power of God.

The hope and ideal of many Christians is seen somewhat in Kingfish Ben Cohen. Cohen is a young Negro who runs a junk business in Philadelphia. Several years ago, the Kingfish began wondering what he could do to help revive his North Philadelphia neighborhood and to blunt the cycle of poverty and violence that had turned other urban ghettos into racial powderkegs. He had no use for either the buttoned-down white bureaucrat with his War on Poverty nor for the radical black power advocate with his gospel of hate. Spending a lot of money or blowing up buildings were the easy ways. What ghetto youths needed, he decided, was a place of their own.

So he started a club in the first floor of his home and began inviting members of the powerful North Philadelphia youth gangs. Soon he had to move his family out to make room for all the members.

The club embarrassed the NAACP by calling itself the Knights of the Mystic Sea, after the lodge in the old "Amos 'n' Andy" show. The NAACP had condemned the show as degrading the Negro race. The Knights didn't care. They were having some fun with their image. They were seeing the things that seemed important to them and maintaining their independence.

And the Kingfish helped them. He talked them out of rioting in the summer of 1967. He helped them start their own businesses. He made them proud without any white charity or black hatred.

Some Christians reject the whole idea of Christian social action. This third group sees social action as a hypocritical attempt to smuggle non-Christian ideas into Christianity, thereby making it more palatable to a world which no longer has the moral courage to be Christian. When Christians begin accepting people like the Berrigans, says the more conservative Catholic, they ignore all the lessons which twenty centuries of Christianity have taught — the inability of sinful man to change society radically for the better, the necessity of political power to curb man's desires and passions. Let Christians follow the traditional practice of goodness and charity toward individuals, says this third group, rather than some vague meaningless goal of "social justice." Let Catholics embrace loyalty to Holy Mother the Church and not hand her over to the shouters of revolutionary slogans.

These are only three very general Christian outlooks toward reform. Actually, the number of positions is almost limitless. And there is no easy way of deciding whose position is most Christian. In the final analysis what a Christian must do is use his God-given practical reason, in the light of Christian insight and Church teaching, to arrive at reasonable decisions about what he or she can actually do to relive human suffering.

Must the Christian be a leader in the work of social reform? Must he become personally involved in this work even when he has little personal talent for it?

Here again there is no pat answer. On the one hand, it is clear that people have a wide variety of personalities and talents. So individual Christians cannot be conveniently pigeonholed as "leaders" or "followers." On the other hand, the Gospels tell us that the Christian is somehow responsible for seeing that the lives of the people around him are made as human as possible. At the very least, this means that the Christian should see that his own life and activities do not hinder the humanization of other people.

So there is a constant tension in every Christian's life between his own personality, interests, and aspirations, and those of others. Often, each Christian is like Christ in the Garden of Gethsemane. He is torn between concern for himself and responsibility toward others.

How can an individual personally determine the best way to fulfill his Christian responsibility to others?

There are two basic ways: (1) by understanding his own personality, the circumstances in which he finds himself, and the particular talents and shortcomings that are part of his makeup; and (2) by opening himself to the call of God's grace, which is always attempting to lead him to a fuller, richer Christian life.

Every person has a certain potential. Society does not expect a small-town businessman or a big-city worker to negotiate nuclear test-ban treaties. At the same time, a diplomat might be completely helpless if he tried to cope with the hundreds of little worries and responsibilities involved in running a small business. Human life has become far too complex for any one person to be able to list the activities and occupations of his fellow men, much less take part in them.

At the same time, being conscious of our limitations is no excuse for being passive. Christians believe that men are instruments of the Holy Spirit in the humanization of man. The power at work here is God's power, and Christians are always encouraged to be open to the inspiration of the Holy Spirit, to be ready, like Abraham, to go forth into an unknown land, relying only on a word of promise.

There is no easy way of reconciling a person's own ideas on what he can do with what the Spirit wants him to do. There is no easy way of separating divine inspiration from personal emotion, prejudice, or even fanaticism. People can only try to remain free and open enough to be ready in case the Spirit calls them to do a new thing in his name.

Discussion

1) Are there things an American housewife or working man can do about the Vietnam war, racial prejudice, urban riots, poverty in America, open housing laws, or high food prices in ghetto areas? Do you think these matters should be the concern of every Christian? But what can one Christian do alone? Do individual Christians feel frustrated about their inability to *do* anything? Or is this claim of powerlessness just a cloak for unconcern, apathy, a lack of true Christian charity? To what extent can a city council or state legislature solve such problems as narcotics addiction? inadequate housing? unemployment?

2) Does Christ strike you as a "practical man"? Was it practical to take up the cross and die when he could have escaped? Was deciding to forego marriage for the sake of others practical? Does it make sense to sell all you have and give to the poor? What is the relationship between your personal ideals and ambitions and Christ's call to true social responsibility?

3) Do you know people who are "Christian" only on Sunday? Does modern society make it more difficult to be a Christian during the week than it was in Christ's time? Give examples of things or situations which make it harder (or easier) for modern man to be a Christian. How can a man possibly be a Christian in the dog-eat-dog business world we know today? Increasingly common is the person who accepts "gifts" for favors, cuts corners on his responsibilities, cheats his employer on everything from paper clips to expense accounts. How can an individual fight the pressures on him to do the same? Did Christians of your parents' generation face problems like these?

Do your ideas about the needs of society agree with those of the commentators you read in the newpapers or watch on television? Do your ideas agree with those of high school and college students you have talked with? Do your ideas agree with the ideas in the various social encylicals? Do you think most Catholics are familiar with the Church documents mentioned in the discussion? If not, what reasons can you give for this?

How is it possible that some Catholics are very conservative on political and social matters, while others are liberal and even radical? Is this split possible because Christian doctrine allows for very broad interpretation? Because Christian doctrine really has nothing to do with political and social matters? Or for some other reason?

Do you really believe that there is any connection between social action and the faith you have known all your life? In your own life, do faith and social action ever come into contact?

4) What are some of the implications of Christian social teaching for Catholic education in today's world? What values can a Christian education have in a society full of change and innovation, in a society in which fixed traditions and standard ideas no longer apply? Has Catholic education ever functioned as anything other than a protector of tradition? Will Catholic education be able to survive the drastic changes now occurring on the American scene? Is it really worth spending so much money for Catholic education?

5) List the good and bad points of organizations in your parish or community set up in response to specific social needs, for example, parish ecumenical and interracial societies. Block committees to improve neighborhoods? Other groups? Do you think that increased Catholic membership in these organizations would help improve them?

Possibility
and
Promise

chapter 7

Christianity Means Hoping

The Need for Hope

Dickens wrote in the opening section of *A Tale of Two Cities*, "It was the best of times, it was the worst of times, it was the age of wisdom, it was the age of foolishness, it was the season of Light, it was the season of Darkness, it was the spring of hope, it was the winter of despair, we had everything before us, we had nothing before us, we were all going direct to Heaven, we were all going direct the other way. . . ." That was in 1859.

More than a half century later, in 1922, T. S. Eliot wrote in his poem "The Waste Land": "Unreal City,/Under the brown fog of a winter dawn,/A crowd flowed over London Bridge, so many./I had not thought death had undone so many./Sighs, short and infrequent, were exhaled/And each man fixed his eyes before his feet."

In 1922 Europe was littered with the smoldering wreckage of World War I. "The Waste Land" reflected the sense of alienation and loss that came out of the war. It quickly became a classic for that embittered time. And like all great classics, its melancholy message is, unfortunately, as current today as it was nearly 50 years ago. For

today we recognize World War I as the first of our great modern wars, and rather primitive combat at that.

The plaintive songs of Bob Dylan and other modern-day folk-singers express the same sense of grieving and loss of hope. Dylan sings of standing in front of a "dozen dead oceans" or walking "ten thousand miles in the mouth of a graveyard." He predicts the suffering and hurt that is still to come, when he murmurs: "It's a hard rain gonna fall." Simon and Garfunkel tell it the same sad way. In his "Music from Big Pink," Richard Manuel agonizes over our insensitivity to the hopelessness of life: "Isn't everybody dreaming?/Then the voice I hear is real./Out of the idle scheming,/Can't we have something to feel?"

Many may feel that the drummer to whom the turned-on generation marches is really an escaped lunatic banging on a tin plate with a spoon. But there is no denying the power and feeling of that generation's message. Hope they are saying to us, has almost gone out of style.

And its absence has given society that sagging look of an alcoholic who is half on and half off the bottle. Everywhere we look there is trouble — in Africa, Asia, Europe, Latin America; in our schools, our ghettos, our factories, our cities, our politics, our families, our Church. Newspapers, magazines, and television spoon out a numbing diet of war, violence, crime, and injustice. Our art no longer strives for beauty but for "truth" in a Campbell's soup can, comic-book blow-ups, garbage sculptures, and anything else that captures the banality and worthlessness of existence. Playwrights like Edward Albee hold that we all "feed on the calamities of others." They see modern society as having mechanized and pulverized our individuality and convictions, producing the so-called "organization man."

Hope is simply not popular today. Cynicism and despair are the watchwords — even when it comes to the current revolution rocking the Church. But despite all these problems and difficulties, or perhaps because of them, the Christian who digs into the resources of his faith can recover an attitude of hope; and he can express it. His whole approach to life is founded, after all, upon a theology of hope.

What is meant by a theology of hope? How would a person whose religion was founded on a theology of hope think and act?

A theology of hope is a theology that looks forward to the future with a new kind of realism, a new way of assessing what is happening in the world.

If "The Waste Land" mourns the death and disease of the present day, a theology of hope points toward a sense of risen life today and tomorrow, toward patterns of promise. Hope affirms that God is striving for the redemption of mankind. Jesus was — and is — God's son. Jesus lived in an inhuman world. He died most cruelly. But he rose from the dead and sent his Spirit to us. And his Spirit is active in human life today to help the human race grow toward its full and rich potential, into the complete humanity of Christ.

All this — and much more — is the foundation of a hope theology. A theology of hope, says the German Lutheran theologian Jürgen Moltmann, provides a "thermal current of hope in all articles of the Christian faith." One key to understanding a hope theology is to recognize the "pull of the future." Although every basic statement of Christianity "feels" that pull, theology of hope focuses on the future; and, considering the "pull of the future," it takes a new look at every part of the Christian faith.

For example, even the simple statement, "God exists," enjoys a special understanding in a theology of hope. God is not the kind of God with whom most Christians of today are familiar. God is not, as Carl Braaten put it, "most at home in the past." He does not relate to the present only through the churches. He does not keep his distance from those revolutionary tendencies in society which accept responsibility for the future. God is not afraid of revolution. He is not busy trying to protect the "social status of Christianity."

A theology of hope knows God is intensely involved in human lives. He fills the world with promise, and he always keeps his promises. He directs and channels human energies toward a future world he is even now in the process of creating. The purpose of a theology of hope, Braaten suggests, is to help "man's hopes burst open his present, connect him with his past, and drive him toward the horizons of the . . . future."

A New Outlook — Hopeful and Frightening

Concerned with possibility, promise, and the insistent pull of the future, a theology of hope may result in some rather unsettling changes. The bishops at Vatican Council II recognized the need for these changes: "Today's spiritual agitation and the changing conditions of life are part of a broader and deeper revolution. . . . History itself speeds along on so rapid a course that an individual person can scarcely keep abreast of it. The destiny of the human community has become the same for all. . . . The human race has passed from a rather static concept of reality to a more dynamic evolutionary one."

Changing from a somewhat static view of religion to a dynamic, future-minded view is no simple matter. As Mark Twain once noted, habit "is not be be flung out of the windows by any man — it must be coaxed downstairs a step at a time." People may be open to change, may even approach change with great hope and expectation, but they still cannot escape a sense of unease and nervousness. Old habits and thoughts, like favorite old bedroom slippers, are hard to throw out.

On the eve of his marriage a young man may be filled with love and expectation. But he also may be a little scared. He has never had to share himself with anyone before. There will be another person's health and happiness to worry about. He begins to feel the heavy responsibility. He realizes that he will have to alter the whole inner landscape of his ideas and consciousness. He may even begin to wonder whether marriage is really worth it.

On the eve of his retirement, a man whose life is largely behind him may feel the same heaviness. For years he has looked anxiously forward to the day when he could say goodbye to that nine-to-five grind, when he could catch up on those books he has wanted to read, do the fishing he wanted to do, see those wonderful, far-away places the airline ads talk about. But as retirement draws near, he becomes acutely conscious of those lonely-looking old men sitting on front porches or park benches — saying nothing, doing nothing, looking at the world with sad, empty eyes. And he wonders: What am I going to do with all the time? Will I really enjoy myself? Will there be anyone who really needs or wants my company? Or will I be just another piece of furniture that my daughter has to move when she's cleaning?

Sometimes, the problem goes far beyond the fear of new experiences and habits. Some people simply refuse to believe that the world has changed, that the car has replaced the horse, the light bulb the gas lamp, the transistor the vacuum tube.

To these people, the old way of doing things is the only way.

Any new approach is unnatural, degrading, and perhaps even a trifle perverted. What they refuse to accept is that the world has been in a state of continual change since the dawn of time; today's frontiers become tomorrow's way stations. And as technology races off into whole new spheres of research and exploration, the rate of change can only speed up, thus expanding our knowledge and learning.

In reality they share the same fears and resistance to change that we all instinctively feel. The difference is simply one of degree. There is no easy way to make men do the right thing when it is not what they are used to doing. People are continually being drawn outward by their hopes for the future and pulled back again by fears of the new and unfamiliar.

As people begin new ways of life, fears and misgivings are natural. But fear need not stop them from setting out upon new adventures and approaches to life if they seem worthwhile, valuable, and attractive. Two young people who want to get married are willing to change their way of life and overcome their fears. An oldster who feels that retirement opens whole new vistas of experience and accomplishment is willing to "shift gears" in his ways of living. Part of what makes us unique as human beings is our willingness — when it seems important to us — to rearrange our lives, habits, and emotional patterns.

"The Land Which I Will Show You"

Abram was just another unimportant desert chieftain when God said to him: "Depart from your country and your relatives and your father's house and go into the land which I will show you. I will make of you a great nation, I will bless you, and make your name great." Abram never hesitated a moment. He went as the Lord commanded. He never doubted that with God's help he and his descendants would do great things.

When God summons men in the Bible, he makes nothing easy for them. Abraham (this was his new name) had to show his faith in God by leading his family, servants, and flocks across hundreds of miles of wilderness and desert, with no clear notion of where he was going. It was a time of upset and turmoil, and the settled communities through which he passed felt no particular love for a wandering patriarch and his clan. His hope in God was stretched to the breaking point when God commanded him to sacrifice his only son, Isaac. How could his race be great if he had no descendants to carry on? But Abraham never gave up hope in the promises God made to him.

Nor were Jacob and Joseph, Moses and Joshua, Samuel and David, Isaiah and Jeremiah, and the other heroes of the Old Testament called to an easy life. Like a plant pulled up by its roots, they were wrenched from the comfortable soil of routine, as soon as they agreed to do God's work.

Jesus' call to the apostles was equally demanding. He walked into their lives and told them to follow him. He called them to a style of life entirely different from fishing, farming, or tax-collecting. But he did not wait around for them to test the water and ease themselves into the new routine. He expected them to plunge in and leave everything behind to follow him. There was no time for peace or comfort; he brought not peace, but a sword.

To be a disciple of Jesus, a man had to be ready to change radically his way of living and thinking. One famous example occurs in the story of the rich young man who said to Jesus: "Teacher, what must I do to have eternal life?" And Jesus replied: "If you want to be perfect, go and sell your possessions and give the money to the poor, then come and follow me."

Becoming a good Christian involves ending an old way of life and abruptly taking on a new one. But becoming a Christian is a never-ending task. A Christian is always in a state of becoming. At times, this involves pain, disruption, dislocation. Often these are inescapable if we are to do what needs to be done.

Possibility and Promise

"God keeps his promises." That is the great "bridge idea" between the two Testaments of the Bible, according to many modern biblical experts. It is also the foundation for Christian hope.

Paul on trial in Caesarea said: "I am standing trial now for hope in the promise made by God to our fathers." Paul is a Christian who, reaching back into ancient times, puts his hope in the belief that promises made to the Old Testament patriarchs are fulfilled in Christ. This way God's promises can be seen as a bridge from the Old Testament to the New Testament. Hope is the bridge.

But hope is more than a bridge to the past. It is also a bridge to the future, since many of God's promises still stand. One such bridge is God's ancient promise to send a Messiah. Jesus, of course, is the Messiah. And he came among men and returned to the Father. But in another sense he has still to come in the full human growth of each human being. A second bridge to the future is Jesus' promise to send his Holy Spirit. Historically, the Spirit came to men on Pentecost but he is still with us according to Jesus' promise, to inspire every human being to grow in truth and love. Hope finds another bridge in Jesus' promise to return to earth at the end of time to establish his kingdom once and for all. Christians today can be concerned with the enormous human possibilities of the future because their lives are lived in the light of God's promises, his faithfulness, and his forgiving love. In the Old Testament God proved his own faithfulness by blessing Abraham and the patriarchs with children, safety and finally a land of their own. He did this despite the unfaithfulness of his people. His promises penetrated into the New Testament with the coming of the Messiah and with the beginning of the reign of God in the world. To complete what remains of remolding the world under God's gracious hand constitutes "the pull of the future." There is work to be done and a world to be shaped and kneaded into a new creation. This new creation is already promised by God in Christ. It is the work of God, in which human beings participate.

The Challenge of an Active God

Will this hope-centered view of religion demand that some people change both their attitude toward God and their understanding of him?

In the hope-centered approach to religion, there is certainly a different emphasis and perspective than in some of the traditional approaches. Christian faith, for example, has always taught that God is all-powerful, infinite, eternal, and all-knowing. But Christian hope stresses a personal and dynamic understanding of God; it focuses on his continuous involvement with mankind rather than on an abstract definition of his being or an itemization of his qualities and powers. In this it follows Scripture, which draws a vivid and dynamic picture of God in both the Old and New Testaments.

For the Hebrews, God is always active. He is the God who goes before his people wherever they travel and keeps them from harm. He is personally and profoundly involved with his people. He is always preparing good things for them. He agonizes when they fall away from him. He rejoices when they respond to him and what he is trying to do for them.

Jesus himself speaks of God as being actively and energetically involved with men. The God of whom he speaks is doing a new thing for his people. He is transforming and renewing the world, purging it of sin, and building his kingdom among all men.

A certain inescapable risk is taken by people who take this Scriptural view of God, which is the view of the hope theology of today. It is a rich and enriching, "mind-expanding" view; but once a person starts thinking of God in active terms, he may start thinking about his own part in God's work in active terms. He may no longer be satisfied with just going to Mass and obeying the ten commandments. His realization that people are called to work with God in remolding the world may lead him to see that legal and formal obedience are no longer enough. Of course, legal and mere outward obedience were never enough, but this was never so clear before.

The Christian who takes God's activity seriously must follow Abraham along a road, leading to a distant destination. What he needs to bear in mind is that God's calling is no mere byroad, but the highway to a fuller, richer life. Mistakes and failure lurk like great chuckholes along the way, and the signposts are not always clear. But it is not man who called God; it is God who called man. And when God calls, questions of familiarity and habit must take a back seat to the work which he is accomplishing.

Doesn't this view create confusion and doubt rather than hope? Won't people take the Church into their own hands, and won't their prejudices ruin its work?

Certainly a dynamic view of God is challenging and risky for the institutional Church, as well as for the individual. And doubtless this spirit of freedom and change will seem to threaten at times. For always freedom implies doubt. Freedom implies the possibility of being mistaken as well as correct, of being frightened as well as confident, of being doubtful as well as certain. The source of true unity among Christians, however, does not lie in any similarity of ideas or words or institutions, though these may well be valid expressions of unity. The true unity of the Church comes from the Holy Spirit whom Christ sent and is still sending from the Father.

Christian unity is a gift of God to his people, not something that men and women achieve on their own.

How can we be sure that all this "future" business is not just an illusion?

Christianity was born in the hope that God was doing a new thing. The new creation which Paul anticipated was no mere continuation of the old ways. It was a radical innovation, a new way of looking at things and doing things. Jesus himself talks about the coming time when the kingdom of God will burst into the everyday world; so it is clear that he is looking forward to a change that will go to the very roots of mankind and the world.

Yet Christians have every right to be careful about what innovations they embrace. An essential of Christian doctrine is that no mere human thing can be entirely good. Evil touches everything in the world. In every change there may be loss as well as gain. Prosperity and a rise in the Gross National Product may bring inflation that eats away the precious savings of an elderly couple. A new piece of labor-saving IBM equipment may mean that scores of unskilled laborers will be put out of work. We have, in our own way, sacrificed a mountain of human flesh and bone to our bridges, skyscrapers, airliners, and space ships.

In and of itself human talent can find no lasting way out of the nets of misery and evil. Confusion, conflict, misunderstanding, physical pain will always keep cropping up like weeds in a lovely garden. The Christian believes that only God can solve the basic problems of human existence. But he also believes that God wants us to work with all our hearts to help achieve this solution. He has commanded us to do what we can to eliminate suffering and evil, to make the world more human. And he has promised that our efforts, no matter how puny and failure-ridden they seem, will not be in vain.

Where did God command us "to make the world more human"? What do you mean "more human"?

God's command that men "make the world more human" is not a command like one of the ten commandments of the old Mosaic Law. Nor is it be be found in Jesus' sermon on the mount in the New Testament. Rather, it is implied throughout the New Testament, on almost every page. When a person receives a book as a gift, he does not need to be told to read it. The same applies to life itself. Man needs the commandment to live as fully as possible, as humanly as possible. "I came that they may have life and have it more abundantly," said Jesus. That — and many other statements of his — implies his concern that life be more human. His followers have always felt that they should do the same. It is through Christian labor which makes the world and the people within it more human that we see the ongoing fulfillment of God's promise in Ezekiel: "I will give you a new heart and put a new spirit within you, and I will take away your heart of stone and will give you a heart of flesh."

Anytime people help improve the quality of life — intellectually, economically, politically — they help render the world more human. Even man's molding, probing, and "working" of the earth, his conquest and use of matter itself, is a contribution toward the humanizing of creation.

Don't the enemies of Christianity often use "progress" as a substitute for God? Doesn't this kind of tactic make it unwise for the Church to talk of progress? Surely the Church should not abandon God to chase after the idols of secular humanism.

Certainly, people have frequently tried to substitute a religion of progress for a religion of God. But this is no reason for the Church to abandon its obligation to discuss the relationship between progress and God's promise of salvation. Vatican II reminded us that the Church has a great deal to learn from non-Christian sources. One of the things the Church can learn from secular humanism is a proper regard for the importance of human purpose and human progress.

Doesn't the 1968 creed of Pope Paul imply rejection of this kind of program? This reaffirmation in the creed of traditional Catholic teaching — isn't this a rejection of radically new approaches to the mysteries of faith?

A Catholic believes in the truth of the doctrines of faith Pope Paul enumerated. But this belief is only the beginning. Not content with abstract formulations, the Christian goes on to expand his understanding of doctrine and to relate it to all his life experiences. This focus on hope is just such an effort at expanding and enriching an understanding of doctrine. It is in the tradition of St. Augustine's famous formula: "I believe in order to understand." It is meant to be an example of St. Anselm's idea of theology as "faith seeking understanding."

Dogma is the basic focus, the bare minimum. Our minds are of God's creation. All are expected to use all the powers they have to go beyond bare minimal understanding. Christ spoke of loving God with "all your heart and mind and strength." We can't do this without *thinking*.

Christianity Means Responsibility

A Sense of Concern

Today people are intensely concerned with their responsibilities to others. This concern extends across political and religious boundaries. Left, right, and center, Protestant, Catholic, and Jew are all concerned with their obligations to one another and to other men.

A good example is the attitude of many Negro celebrities toward other members of their race. Basketball star Lew Alcindor, for instance, was extremely sensitive to the fact that "all those kids in the ghettos" look up to him. He has spent summers working with ghetto kids, believing that he could accomplish far more good than any professional social worker, because of his towering prestige in the sports-minded black community.

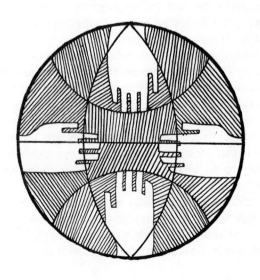

At one time, no one expected a Negro celebrity to care that much about less fortunate Negroes. And few did care. But today many wealthy and successful Negroes feel a strong sense of concern and responsibility for the welfare of their race. Their contribution goes beyond giving financial support to civil rights groups and other organizations. Their concern involves a conscious recognition that they are the symbols of the black race for both white and black, goodwill ambassadors between the two cultures. They feel that the white man's respect for the black, and the black's respect for himself, are deeply bound up with the lives and actions of famous Negroes who have made it.

Conservative politicians and theorists have always been suspicious of the strong humanitarian claims of the leftists. They tended to feel that left-wing concern for the downtrodden was really only a smokescreen for the left's political ambitions and an excuse for the increased government intervention which conservatives oppose. In recent years, however, more and more conservatives have decided that human welfare should not be sacrificed at the altar of left-right political squabbling. If there are real needs which are not being filled, there is need, they say, for government support and intervention. An example of this changed attitude is expressed in an address given by conservative spokesman William F. Buckley to the Conservative Party of New York. He stated:

"What needs to be said [about Negroes in the United States] is something of the following order: (1) the Negroes in the United States, and in Harlem, suffer from accumulated indignities and privations which we as white people are to a considerable extent responsible for. We need to go on to say, (2) we are required to believe, as conservatives who accept the fact of the brotherhood of man because we are creatures of God, that the Negro is in the most important respects the equal of every one of us. We must say, (3) that inasmuch as it is the case that the Negro is especially disadvantaged in our society as a result of his oppressive legacy, then it is our duty to do what we can to liquidate those artificial disadvantages."

College students have also become more acutely aware of their responsibilities here. Ten years ago the volume of college-based educational and charitable work was almost negligible. Now student involvement is at an all-time high. Students are running recreation programs, tutoring backward or especially promising children, helping ghetto residents repaint and repair their neighborhoods. Many students are devoting their academic careers to the study of poverty, inadequate housing, and all the other social evils that afflict the underprivileged.

There is, of course, no guarantee that these or any other well-intentioned efforts will pay off. At the same time that black people are trying to raise themselves out of despair, black-power racists and fanatics threaten to undo everything with their preachments of hate and violence. Expensive government poverty programs may also end up saddling us with a vast, cumbersome poverty bureaucracy which exists for its own sake more than for the poor. Much of the college social action may also be just a way of salving one's middle-class sense of guilt, thus benefiting the students more than the poor. But the expanding sense of human responsibility, whatever its motives and shortcomings, seems a good and admirable thing — especially when one considers the alternatives.

Active Lord, Active Servants

"This is my commandment, that you love one another as I have loved you."

Jesus made it clear that he expected a great deal from his disciples. "He who is greatest among you shall be your servant: whoever exalts himself will be humbled, and whoever humbles himself will be exalted." He also made it clear how he expected his disciples to exert themselves: in love and service, in justice, mercy and faith. Loving and helping other men is an inseparable part of loving God. Jesus did not try to hide the fact that this would be hard work. He compared the love and service that he expected from his disciples to the way men labor in everyday life. Like servants of a master, they are expected to return a master's gifts with compound interest. Like the trees in a profitable orchard, they are expected to bear good fruit.

What Jesus demanded of his disciples takes on a clearer meaning if we look at the people he attacked. It is important to recognize that the Pharisees were not evil people. In fact, they were among the most upstanding of men. But Jesus was brutal in his condemnation of them, while at the same time forgiving all manner of sinful and disreputable ne'er-do-wells.

"Woe to you, scribes and Pharisees, hypocrites," Jesus said, "for you tithe mint and dill and cummin, and have neglected the weightier matters of the law, justice and mercy and faith; these you ought to have done, without neglecting the others. You blind guides, straining out a gnat and swallowing a camel."

The reason for his severity was simple. The Pharisees were so impressed with their own goodness that they forgot that what they are and have is a gift of God, that the response God asks of them is a life of love and service to other men. They are content with following the traditional doctrines, ideas, and rituals. They completely overlooked that vital element in Christian faith: God's activity in the world. They forgot, as well, his call to men to take some part in that activity.

Man's role in God's activity is important. But we must not fool ourselves into thinking that our activity has any meaning apart from God's activity. "Without me you can do nothing." Nevertheless, God's power does not exempt man from trying to make man more human. The very fact that Jesus came among us as another man shows that man's part in creating a new heaven and earth is of great importance.

And the part that Jesus calls Christians to carry out is no fuzzy humanitarianism, no vague, hippy-style, universal love. Jesus says: "If you love me, you will keep my commandments." There is no love of God apart from good works toward other men. As the first letter of John says: "If any one says, 'I love God,' and hates his brother, he is a liar." When people try to become sentimental about him and his mission, Jesus brings them sharply back to earth: "As he said this, a woman in the crowd raised her voice and said to him, 'Blessed is the womb that bore you . . .' But he said, 'Blessed rather are those who hear the word of God and keep it.'"

Salvation and Christian Responsibility

How does God want an average person to respond to him and do his work — an average person for whom it is a struggle to save his own soul? What can he do to help shape the future? He's not a revolutionary but just an ordinary person.

The idea of saving one's soul, as expressed above, is too narrow to be any longer acceptable as a basic Christian idea. The word *soul* is not, in fact, a proper translation of what the Gospel says.

Soul is a later concept and is philosophical language. The Gospel speaks rather of "saving one's *life*," a far more total and more "worldly" idea.

What Christianity is all about is what God is doing in the world and how persons are involved in it. One of the important things God is doing is his promise to his people for a transformed *human* life after death. But this transformed life is not like a Christmas stocking that a child receives when he is good. God commands us to begin the transformation of human life right here on earth. And perhaps the most important way to begin this transformation is to enrich our relationships with other people.

Are our relationships with others evidence of our Christian love and service? Are they bringing about peace and friendliness and understanding, and thus helping us become more fully human? If not, God commands that they be made to do so, and that we start building our humanity into something worthy of living forever.

Salvation is not something we can get just for ourselves. Our salvation is inseparable from our relation to the rest of mankind. A selfish concern for one's salvation is not genuinely Christian; in a very real sense, it is a refusal to be human, to be a person. It is a movement away from God, a defiance of God's design for human love and mankind's salvation.

Obviously, a person can enter into truly and intensely human relationships with only a small fraction of the people he knows, and certainly not with the whole human race. Christ does not want us to use such limitations as an excuse for doing nothing at all; yet that is precisely what many people do: nothing. Despite many obstacles, we must constantly keep alert to our obligation to become more and more human and also to help others to grow in humanity.

Experience proves that most efforts in the direction of "humanization" have been failures, and one would think that they are likely to go right on being failures. In what sense then can man really be said to be responsible for his own future, given his miserable record to date? Shouldn't final salvation be left in the hands of God?

As Christians, we have God's promise that he will create "a new heaven and a new earth." But the whole point of Christianity is that God has also said that men can join in this new creation. All the humanizing or dehumanizing things that go on in the world are thus either cases of human cooperation with or cases of human opposition to God's shaping of the future. The final achievement of humanity will not occur until Christ comes again. But God creates situations in which men can start working out their humanity.

God's eventual triumph over evil in our world is visible to us only "through a glass darkly." The evils and failures are much more numerous and obvious. But his is no excuse for putting off what can be done now to help make man more human. God always understands and forgives failure; but he never accepts despairing surrender. The Holy Spirit that Christ sends from the Father is always with us; so despite all discouragement, we have every reason to keep trying to make ourselves and others more human.

Talk of Christian responsibility can be very inspiring. The only trouble is that many of the people who preach Christian responsibility are very hard to take. When they talk at parish meetings, for instance, they seem to be smug about how liberated and Christian they are. They act as if only the poor and black are worthy of notice and benevolence. Everyone politically even slightly to the right of H. Rap Brown is treated as some sort of leper.

One of the discoveries of Catholics in recent years is that the Church has a large contingent of left-wing as well as right-wing pharisees. The well-to-do suburban Catholic and the priest working in civilian clothes in a Negro slum may both be sorely tempted to thank God that they are not like the rest of men. Some yield to the temptation all too often. To recognize this is to see in one more way the basic point of Christianity: We are all of us in need of continual reflectiveness, prayer for God's help, an openness to the facts, and, in the end, God's forgiveness for our mistakes and sins.

But the shortcomings of Church renewal are no excuse for breaking off the Christian search for ways of making men more human. There is no excuse either in someone's ducking out because he can't play the guitar or doesn't have the patience to shepherd fifty ragged little ghetto kids on a field trip to the zoo — much less the patience to take a radical student leader or a black nationalist to lunch. St. Paul was well aware that different Christians had very different temperaments and talents. In his first letter to the Corinthians, he said that Christians should be related to each other as the different parts of the body are to the body as a whole. Each should contribute what he can.

In our own day there are many more ways of earning a living

and living a life than there were back then. So St. Paul's message may be even more meaningful now than when he wrote it.

For a Christian, more occupations and the rich variety of life mean more ways of making men more human. Each of us — doctor, lawyer, politician, businessman, journalist, scholar, civil servant, housewife — knows of inhumanities in our life and work which we might be able to transform if we were willing to exert ourselves. Once in a while a few of us are in a position to strike a great blow for humanization. At other times, we could do smaller things that may have no greater impact in the total scale of humanity than making us a few enemies among those who don't care about the human development of man. But even our small efforts are important.

Discussion

1) Do you find it difficult in today's world of confusion and change to be hopeful and optimistic about your life as a Catholic and about the lives of your children and friends? Are there specific things in the Church — in its teaching, in the bishops and clergy, in Catholics as a whole — which discourage you? Or do you just have a general feeling that things in America and in the world are getting worse and there isn't much you can do about it?

2) Is there among the Catholics you know any relationship between religious feelings and feelings of hope for the future? Isn't the God of most Catholics a God of the past rather than a God of the future and of possibilities? Do you think of your Catholic religion as having a hopeful outlook? Is this hope directed toward the human world of living men and women, or is it directed purely to an otherworldly situation?

Does Christian hope seem to provide a better focal point for religion and life than the kind of approach you may be used to? Is it better, for example, than a cyclic kind of life where you fall into sin and ask for absolution, where you slowly increase in grace, or where you see yourself as a single individual relating to a God who will in the end either reward you or punish you?

3) Most people are inclined to live their lives according to habit — not only in religion but in every part of life. They like to find a groove and stay in it. They choose a principle or norm to live by and tend to remain faithful to it. Most people look for security,

not for revolution and change. What is the guiding principle of your own life? Is it security, or change, or something else? Are there any reasons strong enough to make you want to change the way you have been living your religious life? When are you personally most willing, and for whom are you most willing, to depart from your regular routine — if only to try something new once?

4) We sometimes seem to imply that change is automatically something good. Isn't change rather something that can be both good and bad, something ambiguous? How can one build his faith on something ambiguous? For centuries it seemed that among all the religions in the world the Catholic Church was distinguished by unity and unanimity. It was the one religion where all the members thought alike. Why are theologians now so intent on encouraging Catholics to value different viewpoints, to change attitudes, to try new ways of getting involved with the world? What does change in the world have to do with the salvation of mankind? Why should the Church all of a sudden become preoccupied with the "new"? Shouldn't the Church move much more slowly in making changes?

5) Do you ordinarily think of God as a dynamic and active person? If not, how do you think of him? Why do you think of him in the way that you do? Is it because of your personality? Is it because of your education? Do you find the idea of an active God more appealing than your present view?

6) In Old Testament times, God, in fulfillment of his promise, led his people out of Egypt and into Canaan. Where might God be leading people today? Has God made any promises to the American people of today? Is there any way of telling for sure? Did you ever think of the American people as God's people? Are they, really? Do you think that the directon in which American life is headed is a sign that God is leading us? Or are we inhibiting the work of God?

7) If a Catholic begins to orient his life in the way of Christian hope as the book describes it, won't he have to change his attitude and understanding of who God is? Isn't this risky? What does it mean to give up long-cherished notions about God? Won't the changes that the book seems to encourage really create a lot of doubt and confusion, rather than hope? Won't this tend to split the Church rather than unify it? Weaken the Church rather than strengthen it?

8) Do you think that the Church has been justified in its great concern with unity? Do you think the modern de-emphasis on institutional unity will create more bad situations than it solves? Why? What do you think the Church is looking for in its meeting with Protestants and Jews and in having dialogues with Marxists and Communists?

9) Why do you think we waited until the end to discuss the nature of God? Usually, books on theology begin with a study of God and move down to a consideration of man. We seem to have moved in the opposite direction, from man to God. Doesn't this approach run the risk of describing God in terms of men, rather than describing man as God sees him? Don't we end up defining God as man would like him to be, rather than the way he really is?

VIEWPOINTS AND PROPOSALS

appendix A

Thinking About the Church

Unity and Conscience

In the following pages, two Christians, a Protestant and a Catholic, present a personal account of their faith. They write about their childhood and family as well as their present day experiences. They recognize that their early years were vital in shaping many of their later attitudes and thoughts about Christ, the Church, and the Christian life.

If only in his day-by-day living, every Christian renders the same personal accounting of his faith — what he believes, why he believes, and how he lives out what he believes. The two people writing here differ in the "what," "why," and "how" of their beliefs. Both are Christians with strong faith, yet both live with unsolved problems about their faith. Both are still asking questions and looking for answers. Generally, they do not ask the same questions. But even if they do, they don't usually look in the same place for an answer.

A Protestant Viewpoint

I'm a Southern Presbyterian. For centuries my ancestors have lived and died in the South.

From the time I could first write my name, I learned that to be a Southern gentleman was second only to being a Christian — and sometimes that order was reversed.

I still carry the image of Southern womanhood in me. Somehow I still feel that gentlemen should always rise when ladies enter a room, always give up their seats to the weaker sex. With all her excellences, the northern woman never ceases to shock me with her rapid-fire conversation, her easy competence, and her casual obscenities. "Ladies" just aren't like that.

As I grew older, I came to view the Old South as some sort of golden place. I dreamed my way through early adolescence with the daring Civil War blockade runners, thumbing their noses at Yankee warships to speed supplies to a starving South. I relived Pickett's

187

charge at Gettysburg a hundred times. Each time I prayed that they'd make it, and each time I hurt a little more when they went down into the mud under murderous Yankee fire. I was raised on the story of my great-grandfather being driven off his farm in South Carolina during Reconstruction, of how my twelve-year-old grandfather-to-be supported his family by picking flowers and peddling them in a nearby town. My grandmother will never forgive the "damn yankees" for it, and my mother's voice is still edged with bitterness when she speaks of it.

My father's ancestors entered New York with the Dutch in the 1600's. As the English took over Manhattan, my father's people gradually moved inland and then south, into the Virginia hills. But they were concerned with more than moving on when richer land or better opportunities beckoned over the next hill. The Dutch Renaissance and Reformation lay behind them. They had been hammered on the anvil of the same stern Calvinism that led William of Orange against the Spanish. And so they were never quite conquered and brutalized by the land as were so many of the Anglo-Saxon emigres who became the hillbillies. The Lord their God still demanded that they prove their election, that they work out their salvation in fear and trembling, that their learning and their piety as well as their work establish the reality of their salvation.

My mother came from stout Scot-Irish stock on both sides. During the 17th and 18th centuries they migrated to the Piedmont Caro-

linas in great numbers, took hold of the land, and forced it to yield up its treasures, seeing themselves as latter-day Israelites, entering the promised land. They carved out a good rich life in the fertile zone between the sandy coastlands and the rolling Appalachians.

The land, however, could not totally absorb them. They owed their allegiance to God alone and would not bow their knee to a king nor a president in Washington. They crushed the British offensive in the South at the Battle of King's Mountain; they broke with the national Presbyterian General Assembly in 1861, and the scar still remains. During the Civil War they lost countless sons, husbands and fathers. They would obey only what they understood as the will of God, and no assembly of man could make them do otherwise.

These are my forebears. And the South, imagined in its pre-Civil War grace, was my homeland. Until twenty years ago, it was still possible to believe in that homeland. But as I grew older, the great and grievous faults of the South became inescapable. I could not help but notice the numbing poverty, the pathetic ignorance, the bigotry, the anti-intellectualism, the self-righteous regionalism, the soul-deadening injustice to blacks. The land of Jefferson and Washington, Robert E. Lee and Stonewall Jackson, of Christian gentlemen and beautiful ladies had become the land of the Ku Klux Klan and George Wallace, dirty gas stations, greasy barbecue carry-outs, ignorant red-necks, the land of beautiful, frivolous Alabama cheerleaders and poor brutalized Negroes. The shock of this discovery is still with me. And every time I return to the South, it hammers away at me again and again.

As I grew up, I reached out for salvation. I reached toward science, politics, the academics, psychology. I desperately needed something that would lift me out of the slough of guilt and brokenness. How could I become so that I wasn't this way anymore, so that I wasn't a Southerner?

I got nowhere. Like an ugly malignancy, the ambiguity that slowly intruded into my old dreams about the South began showing up everywhere else, too. Scientists, I discovered, were too often involved in things that didn't really matter. They were lost in their own flyspeck worlds, searching for prestige and success, trying to flee the real problems of the world by dwelling on microscopic irrelevancies. And the politicians knew only how to do things, not what to do. With scholars and psychologists, I felt more at home. Then it became clear, even with them, that the beautiful webs that they spun could not really resolve my questions.

It was about this time I went off to college. I had chosen a small liberal arts Presbyterian college that my father, grandfather, and innumerable uncles, and cousins had attended. It was there that I finally had time to think, to try to make sense of the confusion. Several years earlier I had stumbled upon Jean-Paul Sartre and now his cry that there is no meaning in human life except what man himself created appealed to me mightily. Gradually I was drawn to Sartre's far greater predecessors, Dostoevsky and ultimately, Kierkegaard. They had both realized the deadly ambiguity of human society; mankind is shot through with distortion, corruption, and twistedness — even as it aspires toward goodness, perfection, and divinity. Both felt, as well, that any real meaning for life was thereby destroyed — unless God, Yahweh, the Lord of history actually existed.

It was at this point that an aspect of my tradition came to my mind. "God is a Spirit, infinite, eternal and unchangeable in his being, wisdom, power, goodness and truth." Like many another child I had memorized a catechism. Only there had been a difference. My mother and I had spent endless Sunday afternoons debating what the answers meant. And this particular answer had always seemed most important to me. Because if God really ran things, if he really had a plan for the salvation of men, then all the distortion I saw in the world wasn't the last word. God would not ultimately let it destroy us. He had a plan, and he was omnipotent. He had elected us and he would not let us go.

But the crucial question was, how can I know that God exists? What if Sartre was right and there was no God? What would it mean if God did exist? It seemed perfectly obvious to me that many of the traditional ways men said they knew there was a God were faulty. The warming of the cockles of the heart? I once had a similar feeling when I saw the American flag go up. Doubtless the ancient Aztecs felt moved and thrilled as they sacrificed human victims. My training and upbringing? There was no reason my background was any more "true" and less relative than others. The existence of man and the universe? Hume, the English philosopher, destroyed any such hope. And so on down the line. Every avenue of approach to God, every surety of his existence was ambiguous, unsure, indefinite.

This question began to haunt me: how could I know that God exists? In retrospect I can see I was undergoing an "identity crisis." For the first time I was away from the supporting influences of family, church, and long-time friends. I was lonely and, I can see now, I was very much afraid. I was afraid I wasn't anybody, that I had no identity, that there was no "real" me. The fear of death overwhelmed me: I didn't want to go down into that dank chasm of not-being, of coming apart, of ceasing to be me.

And so I threw myself into understanding how God could be, how could I let myself believe in him. It sounds a little silly now, over-dramatic: a freshman in college, undergoing extreme anxiety because he didn't see how he could believe in God. Belief in God seems to be a given; either a person has it or he doesn't. Either way he should just pick up his rucksack and go on about his business. Life is just given. If there is a God, then he will save me. If there is not, then agonizing over it will accomplish nothing. The whole business sounds a little overdone, an adolescent posturing, a romanticizing of the world and of my place in it.

But even in the midst of my posturing, I think there was an important element. For all my emotional excesses and immaturity, I had discovered something. The first inkling of this came when I pledged a fraternity. I had been something of a social outcast during my high school years, and it was immensely flattering when several fraternities sought me out. I hesitated for a while and then pledged after a week or so. Suddenly I was in the midst of friendly and accepting faces, routed out for shower parties. I was watching TV down at the house, undergoing pledge training.

It didn't work out. I probably was too much caught up within myself to fit into the free and easy atmosphere of fraternity life anyway. But another issue came up before I had time to recognize this. My fraternity's national affiliate was, as were all the rest on campus, lily-white. And the first black student in the college's history had entered with my class. He was snubbed. Politely, and devastatingly. I was furious. With the righteous indignation that comes so easily to an eighteen-year-old, I set out to right the wrong. I organized most of the other pledges and threatened a walk-out if the black student wasn't seriously rushed. The "brothers" responded in

shocked surprise. "Well, I suppose we could have him down for
dinner sometime, but the national fraternity would never let us pledge
him. They'd jerk our charter." My revolt collapsed.

I was miserable. I didn't understand why or how, but the fraternity suddenly lost all meaning for me. This was the fraternity
my father had belonged to and loved, at a college founded to the
glory of God and for liberally educated men. And somehow this
ugly thing had happened. My "brothers." A fraternity of Christian
brotherhood. A month later I resigned.

Looking back, I can see I really didn't understand what was
going on. I was angered and hurt by the "Christian" fraternity. But
what had really torn me apart was what it said about me. The reason
I had been horrified and angered was not only that I thought the
Negro freshman should be treated as an equal. The thing that tore
at me was "if they're like this, then who can I be?" If the smartest,
the best-educated, the most congenial, the best-off young Christian
gentlemen in the South (for so all of us modestly saw ourselves)
were like this, then maybe I was too. By quitting my fraternity that
fall of my freshman year, I served notice on the South: "I'm not one
of yours, I will not be as you want me."

But this expanded the fear of not-being-anybody from a mere
chasm to an abyss. If I could no longer identify with my family,
with my church, with my heritage, then who the hell was I? I remember pulling away from the handful of friends that remained,
from my family, even from studying. I cut classes, slept during the
day, and stayed feverishly awake at night — reading voraciously,
walking for miles in the surrounding country, dreaming wild, pas-
sionate dreams of *being*. Not surprisingly I became, in my own eyes,
a sort of Romantic hero — a latter-day Luther. There is something
a little pathetic about that posture, as I look back on it: a gawky,
lonely scared boy, pretending he held within him the nature and
destiny of all mankind. And yet I began to get hold of some important things then. The fatal twistedness, the deadening perversity
of my homeland was pounded home beyond recall. My home, my
people, my heritage didn't understand what I was about and it didn't
even seem to care. I was alone, I was only what I could make
myself. And, painfully, almost beyond my wishes, I began to realize
I really wasn't so hot myself. I probably wasn't another Luther —
I probably wasn't anybody at all. My culture and my efforts were

fatally twisted, they could not grant me being, they only served to thrust me out into the fearsome dark, into the shadow of omnipresent death.

The psychoanalysts say that a fear like this might result from basic insecurity, dating from childhood or even perhaps infancy. There's probably something to what they say. But living is not a secure and safe occupation. Even for the fortunate handful that go through in relative comfort and security, the last worst enemy stands at the end. Perhaps I shouldn't fear death; maybe I wouldn't if I had grown up differently. But I am afraid. Because the world doesn't work right: high school kids get torn up in wars they know nothing about; babies starve before they can focus their eyes; good and sincere men and women are caught up in the dishonesty around them. The world does constantly threaten to tear people apart. How then can I live confidently and securely in this world?

I can't. Even today I know the world could come apart and tear me into shreds. Sometimes this fear mounts in my throat until I think it will overwhelm, until I cannot speak. And yet . . . But I'm hopping ahead of myself.

There was a man I knew while I was in high school. I used to listen to him, even though I never showed him myself. He seemed to know about things. He was a Southerner and knew the South. And yet he seemed to be somebody. I could tell he hurt a lot inside sometimes. But somehow he managed to keep the world together, to be somebody, to be somebody to other people.

And so I went to talk to him during the spring of my freshman year. I tried to tell him how things were, that nothing meant anything any more, that I wasn't anybody and was desperately afraid I wouldn't ever be. I didn't say it this way: I didn't have the words. It came out in little trickles and inchoate mumblings. He listened. And when I seemed to run down, he just sat there for a minute. And then he said, "Yeah, I hear you. I don't expect you are experiencing very much meaning right now." He said some other things, but I don't remember any of them. I remember what it was like. He was sitting on the stone steps of a big old building. It was spring and the grass and trees were green like it never gets up north. And the sky was blue-and-white. I was standing near the steps with my hand on a tree. I sort of hold that time deep inside of me. I think maybe it was the first time I ever knew that somebody spoke to me, the one inside that feels and thinks and hurts, without trying to get me to be some way or do some thing.

I've held onto that time. It hasn't somehow made things right, made the fear go away, let me trust the things that are. But that one time somebody heard me and spoke to me. And later, when I had the words and the courage to ask him he went on listening and talking. We still talk and sometimes I think I hear him too.

But then, after I finished talking to him, I went back to school. And I battered myself against not-being — how could I *be*? Sometimes I still find myself trying to reach across the abyss and get hold of something real and substantial. Gradually I started to realize what it meant to have talked with a real person. It means that somehow he has reached out beyond his own fear, his own not-being. It's not an easy move and it doesn't last. When you don't expect it, there's somebody standing there near you, listening to you and responding. There isn't anybody who can do it very long. Every man is haunted by a dozen demons and there are twenty hidden fiends for every visible one. And all of them are threatening — you aren't, you aren't good enough, you aren't strong enough, you are not really important. These demons cripple us. We spend our lives flailing at them and hitting the people standing around us. There's no way to exorcise them; they just keep coming.

"And Moses said, 'When the people ask me your name, whom shall I tell them that you are?' And the Lord answered, 'I will be with you.'" "And the Word became flesh, pitching his tent among men." "For God so loved the world that he gave his only Son . . ."

I think I have some faint insight into what these words mean. They mean that the Lord our God is always talking to us, that he is always hearing us. For the Lord of Hosts is haunted by no demons and he need not flail at apparitions. He has heard us in our fear and dread so that he came among us, showing us what it meant to hear what somebody else was saying, to speak to him, and to give him being. He heard us and he responded: he became a man who loved us. He loved us — the people we are; loved us for what we are inside. And he gave us life. This is what eternal life is all about: God gives us personhood that cannot be destroyed, dissolved, evaporated into the abyss.

I didn't learn this all at once. I went back to school and went on trying to exist, to be. But gradually I began to realize that this was what Christianity was all about. God gives being to people, he makes them into persons, he will not leave them to flounder.

I think St. Paul thought something like this. And indeed it was through Paul's philosophy that I began to put together my experience of nothingness and my experience of the gift of personal identity. As I pointed out, my forebears had long known of the sovereign and free God. But he was to these Calvinists a jealous God, only electing a few in his inscrutable will. I remember trying to understand this "hard saying." A learned and long dead Presbyterian divine had written a commentary on the Westminster Catechism, out of which I had learned of God and his sovereign will. I don't remember the exact words, but one of his arguments went something like this: If God had not predestined at least some men to eternal life, then it would be possible that nobody would be saved and the whole incarnation would have been for nothing. I remember agonizing over that passage, rejoicing in its assurance and then worrying that it made God into a petty oriental tyrant. But it was not until years later that I was able to make sense of it. God had indeed predestined men to salvation — but not just a few — all men! This is not to say that sin is meaningless. Nor does it mean that men are good: The threat of the void is too real for such a pious saying. But God indeed grants being to men, speaks to them and hears them — in short, loves them. And thus men are granted that precious identity, are given being. I think this is what Paul was pointing toward when he talked of the new spiritual life given men in place of the old fleshly life. As he says in the first part of Romans, men have become so involved in their own twistedness that they are trapped. They are so haunted by their own demons (Paul speaks of being under worldly powers) that they can neither hear nor speak to each other. And, Paul goes on to say, if men were left in that condition, they could die. But Christ Jesus conquered the powers of this world and gave men to be. And so men are set free from their "estate of sin and misery." God "guarantees" their lives to them. As Paul put it in I Corinthians: "If for this life only we have hoped in Christ, then we are of all men most to be pitied. But in fact Christ has been raised from the dead, the first fruits of those who have fallen asleep. For as by a man came death, by a man has come also the resurrection of the dead. For as in Adam all die, so also in Christ shall all be made alive."

And where does this leave me now? I'm not free and creative and open. I'm up tight on my own fears, fears that I hardly can name and yet which twist and push me. I have some strength and too often use it to buttress my being. I hardly ever hear people and scarcely can speak to anyone. And yet this way of life begins to make some sense. There have been times and people I've heard and who have heard me. Sometimes I feel like I have crushed a legion of demons. More than once I've felt God really existed.

Is there then a God? I just don't know. The kinds of relationships and ideas I've been talking about may or may not have anything really to do with him. I don't see any way of establishing whether they do. On the other hand, if God is something like the way I've been talking about him, I don't think he would make his presence clearly known. For, as Dostoevsky said, God desires the free love of men freely given. And what man could act freely if the presence of God were obvious?

Discussion

1) Would you be afraid to discuss religion with a Protestant? Why or why not? Do you think you could agree with a Protestant on any religious topics? What kinds of topics would provoke the most disagreement?

Do you have a Protestant friend whose explanation of his religion would be much the same as the explanation given by the Protestant in the book? What does the Protestant in the book say — or what do you think he would say — about Mass? the sacraments? the pope? papal infallibility? the Roman Catholic Church?

2) Is religion more important in your Protestant friends' lives or in your own? If a Protestant were converting to Catholicism, what are some of the difficulties he might encounter in getting to feel at home as a Catholic? How might he have to change his attitude about church-going? What place does the Bible play in the Protestant's life? What place does it have in the Catholic's life?

3) Can you see some ways in which the Protestant's family background and early surroundings influenced his later understanding of Christianity? Give examples from evidence in the book.

Discuss the family backgrounds of some Protestant people you know. How did their upbringing differ from yours? What are some experiences which were common to both of you?

A Catholic Viewpoint

I am a Catholic priest. The other day I was talking theology with a Protestant. I brought up the topic of the authority of the Church hierarchy conflicting with the freedom of conscience of the individual in the Church. I started to maintain that there could be a creative tension between these two poles of Catholic life. Each time I tried to talk in terms of "both/and" (hierarchy *and* freedom) my Protestant friend insisted it had to be "either/or." "You can't have a hierarchical Church *and* freedom of conscience," he insisted. "How can you accept contradictions like that?"

Though I'm unwilling to admit that these are contradictions, his remark did make me think. There are a lot of things these days that don't fit neatly together. In fact, there is a great deal of turmoil in the Church, and the pope, bishops, and theologians cannot seem to agree on how to react to it. Still, I'm willing to live in the midst of all the change. Why? How do I find that possible? I suppose the answer is written into my background.

I was born into a well-educated Irish Catholic family in Brooklyn. My grandfather on my father's side was an American-born offi-

cial in the post office. Although he had little formal education he seemed to know Shakespeare by heart and even published three slim volumes of poetry and aphorisms when he was in his seventies. The portrait of that goateed gentleman and his handsome wife had a permanent place in our home. Of their seven children, six grew up in the Church and those still alive remain faithful members to this day. The seventh, the oldest and most brilliant, became quietly fed up with Catholicism while an engineering student in an eastern college. He set out to make a million before he was thirty, and he did so, in Texas oil. Now he is a multi-millionaire and a most generous benefactor to education and the arts. He still isn't tempted to become a churchgoer, but he is a tolerant man and respects the faith of his brothers and sisters.

There is a sense in which the faith of my family is defined in relation to that uncle of mine. Long before the phrase was around, he was the successful man in "the secular city," deeply engaged in all the problems of technological society long before most people gave them any thought at all. Neither his "secularity" nor his marital misfortunes prevented the family from seeing this man as a Christian in the true sense. In fact, the general view of the family is: "Heaven isn't worth going to if *he* isn't going to get in." If anyone did, he kept us from being isolated Catholics in Irish Brooklyn.

Though both of my parents had professional degrees, the Catholic part of their education ended after elementary school. My family wouldn't be considered pious, but it did view things in a Roman Catholic context. We attended Mass and went to confession regularly (more frequent confession for the children than for the parents). Now and then, we tried to get a family rosary going (it never lasted too long, and I never went out of my way to encourage it). Magazines like *America*, *Extension* and *Sign* were always on the coffee table. My parents thought *America* was too bland, and *Extension* was witness to my father's inability to say no to salesmen. The movies we saw were invariably those approved by the Legion of Decency, and this is about all I got out of the diocesan paper.

All of this added up to a rather solid Roman Catholic atmosphere. When I went to elementary school, the Sisters (and the occasional lay teacher) joined forces with my parents to see that my central frame of reference was Christian and Catholic. And I believed literally everything the Sisters told me.

My mind took shape in the serenely peaceful days of unchanging and unchallenged Catholic truth. At the center of my world was Jesus Christ, who came on earth, suffered, died and rose again for me individually and for all men. I knew him as the full revelation of the Father's love for men, for he was God's Son and my personal friend. (I don't mean to say that we made much of Sacred Heart pictures, for my parents thought most of them questionable taste.) To continue his presence with men — for he loved all men, not just his immediate followers — Christ sent the Spirit and founded the Church, which took concrete form for me in the parish church down the street. In the Church his teaching had a voice and his presence a body. The sacraments were instituted by him to give grace and to continue through the centuries the healing, redeeming, recreating power of his. It was especially in the Mass — which I always attended on Sundays and holydays of obligation — that he gave, to those who believed in him, the gift of his presence, since under the sign of consecrated bread and wine he was present in reality and substance. I knew that the Mass was the re-enactment in sacramental form of the bloody sacrifice of Calvary that was accepted by the Father. I knew that by attending Mass Catholics were able to join in Christ's perfect worship of the Father and so share in the fruits of his redemption — the forgiveness of sins, new and eternal life in the Holy Spirit.

I learned that a Catholic was nourished not only by the sacraments but by the teaching of Christ. This teaching was first of all preserved in the New Testament, which, together with the Old Testament, was the record of God's involvement with the new and old Israel. (I never read the Bible as a youngster or teenager, however.) This teaching was itself authoritatively interpreted by the *magisterium*, the teaching authority of the Church, which came to me via the crusty tones of our pastor. Partly because they were so distant, I tended to view popes and bishops as saturated with infallibility. They were considered very close to God.

It wasn't simply formal education that shaped my Catholic experience. My whole life-style as a Catholic contributed to my viewpoint. The spirituality that nourished me stressed the presence of Christ in the Church — his presence among the praying people at Mass, in the Eucharist in the tabernacle, in me as I played or meditated alone, in the teaching Church guiding me when the priest or

sister lectured me. This life-style involved the conviction that I had
received the great grace of explicit faith in God's revelation. This
faith might be frail and faulty, but it was a gift not bequeathed to
all, for a reason I could not give. Johnny, my Jewish friend around
the block, and Gary, my Protestant pal across the street, had either
"missed their chance," or else were lost in a vague and formless
imitation of Roman Catholicism.

Thus, even if I didn't often reflect on it, I always had the sense
that I was living out of a wide and deep tradition 2000 years old, a
tradition that supported and educated me, that knew what was in
the heart of man and what God planned for him.

From all this, there grew in me what I would today call a kind
of "incarnational sense." I expect to find the sacred somewhat mixed
with the "profane." I expect to be able to find God in all sorts
of unexpected places and persons, corrupt popes not excluded. This
sense is not uncommon among Catholics: I find it easy to believe
that, just as the infinite God became man, took on human nature,
and remained the infinite God, he is present and acting in the structure of the Roman Catholic Church, filling it with his Spirit (not that
his Spirit isn't acting elsewhere as well) and leading it — with how
many still on board? — safely to the kingdom. It is his presence that
prevents the Church from slipping too far off center, from ceasing
to be his body. This does not mean, however, that the Church cannot "fail" in many respects. But there is the prevailing sense — a
part of faith and, hopefully, not a kind of smugness — that since
God decided to involve himself with men, the Church that proclaims
and celebrates that involvement will also be a credible sign to men of
God's involvement and of his protection. God has freely committed
himself to the institutional Church and I feel I can depend on that
commitment. I suppose this is the basis for my feeling of hope in
the midst of the change that is flooding our world.

Because of my position as a priest, I am asked to answer many
questions regarding the meaning and the effects of the changes taking place in the Church.

What is the change that is taking place in the notion of "Catholic
truth"?

I well remember the days when there were sources in which one
could find quickly and with certainty what Catholicism was all about,
what the teachings of the Church and its discipline were. There was

no doubt that the classical creeds and doctrines defined in councils and papal encyclicals were the expression of the authoritative voice of Christ. The *index* and *imprimatur* expressed the seriousness with which the Church took books. The missal, the Baltimore catechism and, indeed, the entire Catholic school system were, each in its way, an education in the will of God, in worship, knowledge, and life. The Catholic press, the theological manuals, and the Legion of Decency — all helped inform the Catholic, priest or layman.

But it was especially the voice of the pope that was the voice of Christ. Granted that everything he said and wrote was not infallible, yet he was *the* authoritative voice in Catholicism. And when he addressed himself to the whole Church — or even, for that matter, to a group of midwives or scientists — it wasn't simply a theologian speaking. It was *the* teacher of Catholic Christians. An individual bishop, speaking as pastor of his diocese, was also an authoritative voice when his teaching reflected that of the universal Church. And when all the bishops, along with the pope, defined something solemnly in Council, that teaching was infallibly true and immutable. That teaching was also the authentic interpretation of the basic witnesses to revelation, Scripture and tradition.

It's always easier to tell it like it was than to tell it like it is. But everything that used to be a sure, safe point of reference for the Catholic trying to stay afloat in this world is now a point of debate. Scripture and tradition now, since the Council, have certainly come under close examination and discussion. Even the most unconcerned Catholic realizes that recent scriptural scholarship has made enormous advances. We have more information about the composition and history of the sacred texts than was gained in the previous two millenia of study. All this, of course, has created problems. In the past, the magisterium appealed to Scripture in its teaching, and yet a century ago the bishops' knowledge of Scripture couldn't match that of today. This in itself calls for re-examination of past conciliar statements.

The same can be said of a pope's use of earlier councils. The Council fathers defined doctrine in these sessions, and it may have been infallible. But the understanding which a twentieth century pope or a bishop has of the Council of Trent, say, is not necessarily infallible. Many theologians feel that the whole question of infallible understanding of revelation is filled with problems that Vatican I (which defined papal infallibility) did not understand sufficiently.

A Jesuit specialist on Cardinal Newman, Edward E. Kelly, feels that Catholics have just begun to use the insights of contemporary linguistic philosophy in this area. All Christians believe that human language can be the bearer of God's revelation. But how much do we know about human language, its limitations and potentialities? No twentieth century Catholic can speak of infallible definitions of doctrine with the ingeniousness of earlier ages.

One hopeful sign in all the rethinking of the infallibility issue is that the discussion is moving away from the rarified air of technical theology. Theologians are redirecting their efforts in trying to locate both papal infallibility and conciliar infallibility. Today they discuss the topic within Jesus' promise to be unfailingly present with the entire Christian community. This change of direction is doubly hopeful, for theologians seem to be getting to the heart of infallibility when they analyze and talk about the implications of Christ's promise to his followers. This is the "gut issue," since the promise was made to the whole Church, and the *whole* Church will be the context of Christ's revelation. The whole Church includes Protestants who also believe that Christ's promise of fidelity to his Church is irrevocable. (Vatican II views the Church as something wider than the Roman Catholic Church.) Thus, the basic truth in the concept of infallibility can best be uncovered by Catholics and Protestants studying the problem together, even if they differ in interpretation once the basic truth is uncovered. This would require great humility and courage for a lot of Roman Catholic and Protestant churchmen. But isn't that just what the Spirit is willing to offer those who ask?

Why can't this Spirit-consciousness theology get going and unite the Christian churches?

Perhaps it can. Personally, I'm brought up short by the thought that the Roman Catholic Church has a great deal of history behind it. Some of it is distressing and best forgotten. Some of it is decisive and unforgettable, especially the doctrinal formulations of popes and councils. But the Roman Catholic is accustomed to seeing the Spirit's work in the formulation of those doctrines. That is why it was usual for theologians to say that any future formulations in the Church would have to expand and complement the past definitions, leaving them unchanged in their basic meaning. They always felt that once we say that past definitions of the faith can change, we seem to be wide open to all kinds of confusion and disruption, just as in the Reformation.

Can dogmas change, not just in their wording, but in their meaning? Can a statement that was once taken as God's truth later become more an obstacle than a help to being open to the action of the Spirit? Can an infallible statement of an aspect of God's truth change?

Recently, I heard a Catholic layman at a cocktail party say that truth in biblical terms means God's faithfulness to man, not the Greek view of my-mind-really-reflects-reality. He thought this distinction could free us from centuries of scholastic philosophy of truth, and even of dogma. This sounds simplistic, and I got a bit annoyed and said so. But later I asked myself whether we haven't in fact, been too quick to identify human statements and thoughts with God's faithfulness to us. Sure, God's faithfulness manifests itself in what the pope and councils say, insofar as those statements and definitions help avert crisis, clarify the faith of the Church, preserve unity in the Spirit, help men to be open to the grace of God, and so forth. But they certainly do not completely "mirror" God's revelation, encompass it, or tie it down. Rather, they point to it hesitatingly, so that a better way of expressing God's truth, responding to future actions of the Spirit and needs of a later age, is not excluded. And the pattern of change in the Church's understanding of revelation might resemble a zig-zag. After all, the People of God is a pilgrim people, and its understanding of revelation is perhaps just enough to enable it to continue its journey.

Perhaps Gregory Baum's idea is correct: Development of doctrine is not simply a passage from certitude to certitude, but often enough a *conversion* from a narrow view of what God intends for man to a more generous view, for example, Vatican II's view of non-Catholics compared to the harsh view of the Council of Florence. This isn't simply development or evolution, but conversion and outright change. From examples like these, it is apparent that the Church, in spite of its desire to proclaim the intentions of God, can narrow and restrict the expression of those intentions. The Council of Florence may have been needed in its time to meet certain problems. But it has to be surpassed later, just as Vatican II will have to be surpassed because no matter how well Vatican II did in establishing a program of renewal, it was the work of *men* guided by the Spirit. Yet its surpassable aspect takes nothing away from its value. For its time and era, it is a guide for the future. Yet the future is God's, and so it is larger than the Church's expectation. Moreover, the Church at any one moment of its history is a Church of sinners. And this affects, in countless subtle ways, its ability to represent doctrinally what God is doing among men. It affects as well the moral life of its members. *Ecclesia semper reformanda* — the Church always needing reform — is a closer phrase that refers to both life *and* doctrine in the Church.

Will laymen now be able to contribute much to theology?

Not long ago, laymen used to sit back and let the bishop worry about Church doctrine. But Vatican II explodes that view. According to the bishops at the Council, all the People of God share in Christ's prophetic (teaching) office and help develop doctrine by their lives and reflection.

This is a revolutionary idea, but it isn't a brand new concept. The *sensus fidelium*, the Christian's sense of the faith, has been mentioned by Church teaching for a long time, even though relatively modern scholars like Newman really developed the idea.

But here we have a council saying that all Catholics' opinions count in the Church. Theologians look to the time when there will be structures in the Church which allow expression of public opinion, with the result that the Church will take on genuinely democratic features of the world of which it is a part, just as it took on feudal aspects earlier in its history.

Most theologians cannot accept the position of some that the Church should be completely democratic. Public opinion is crucial for helping to determine the faith of the community. But the meaning of revelation is not determined by counting heads. Thus the Roman Catholic Church will always have a hierarchical dimension. There will be a pope and bishops who together are guided by the Spirit to protect and judge the expressions given to the faith of the Church. Only God can judge the faith of the Church. His promise of fidelity to his people manifests itself in those situations in which the bishops meet challenges and seek to express the orthodox faith. An increasing number of theologians see the Spirit's guidance as a negative safeguard: It only guarantees that the bishops in their teaching role will not shake the faith of the Church. There is no guarantee that the pope or bishops will never be wrong in their ordinary teaching — in encyclicals, pastoral letters, and so on.

Why change dogmatic formulas in the Roman Catholic Church? Does it amount to translating old enigmas (the Trinity, original sin, grace, heaven, purgatory) into bright new puzzles?

Some recent theology would make one think so. But anything that theologians can say to rid Catholics of the idea that the Trinity is the ultimate heavenly puzzle will be magnificent. The Trinity might then once again assume the role it has in the early centuries of the Church.

The doctrine of original sin, as taught to Catholics, has seemed more primeval history than theology, belonging more to the "Department of Curious and Obscure Facts" than to the Catholic's interpretation of himself and his history. If the teaching on original sin can make a difference in our lives, it is when the teaching is viewed as a permanently valid insight into human existence that will help prevent Catholics from becoming utopians.

Again, our dogmatic understanding of the sacraments can make real difference in our lives, if that understanding accents our deeply human roots. It should also make it clear that the People of God have a great deal to do with shape and experience of the sacraments. The doctrine of the Eucharist, for example can make a difference if it takes into account the way people eat their meals, what a get-together means, and how people celebrate and commemorate. In the sacraments the initiative is God's. But the sacraments are liturgy; they are the Church's prayer. Thus, they are more genuinely symbolic when they really express "where men are" before God. This means that the culture and circumstances of contemporary man should form the context in which the Eucharist is celebrated.

Good doctrine, then, can make a difference. It can guide, direct, enlighten, and unravel our experience — when it's good. But where will this meaningful doctrine come from?

The sooner our new young lay theologians come out of the universities, the quicker the average Roman Catholic will realize that theology is not meant to be the almost exclusive concern of "clerics." At the same time, he will also see the tremendous contribution that all people in the Christian community can offer, according to their capacity and degree of involvement. But the participation of more and more people in the process of theologizing will mean even more

varieties of theology in the Church. Until recently, Catholics often
seemed to think that major theological differences of opinion were
found only in the classic struggle between Dominicans and Jesuits,
Thomists and Scotists, and so on. No theological system gave much
attention to the possibility — to say nothing of the *desirability* —
of theological pluralism in the Church.

This, of course, is changing rapidly. Scholastic philosophy and
theology have ceased being the fountainhead of intellectual nourish-
ment, and more and more Catholic theologians are turning to the
different kinds of contemporary philosophers for the rational ground-
ing of their theological investigations. Thus, laymen are being asked
to be more discriminating and critical in their reading, studies, and
even in listening to sermons. The sources for the average Catholic's
view of Christianity are many — teachers, books, magazines, pam-
phlets, sermons and discussions. However, these alone do not present the pure essence of basic truths, nor a core that anyone can
"possess" or understand in its naked state.

Whenever I hear a Catholic pleading for a simple list of basic
truths that he must believe in order to be a Catholic, I'm struck
by his unspoken assumptions that a few phrases presented without
interpretation can be sufficient for any Catholic, that the relationship of the various truths can go unstudied, that the phrases themselves are pure "dogma," containing no human theology. These are
all questionable assumptions.

Even Pope Paul's *Credo*, which was sincerely designed to quiet
the fears of restless and disturbed Catholics, cannot stand alone, independent of interpretation and analysis. Of each phrase, one must
ask, in the light of Christian faith, "What does this mean? What does
this mean to me?" No doubt any pope would be the first to admit
that a creed cannot take the place of Christian education, a theological education.

Will the day come when there will be room for dogmatic differences inside the Church? Granted that there is and will be an increasingly wide variety of theological opinions in the Church, is it
possible that there will also be dogmatic differences? That is, will
it someday come about that the African Church or the Asian Church
will, in local synods, formulate statements which — while not bind-
ing on the whole Church — will be authoritative for and adjusted
to the local Church?

This seems quite likely. These statements could reflect philosophical and cultural differences, and would speak of Christ and the sacraments and the Church in terms that do not simply echo American or European styles of thinking. Obviously, there could not be real disunion or clear contradiction between the teaching of these various regional Churches. But they could exhibit genuine differences of emphasis and attitude. There is a precedent for this — the differences between the Roman and Eastern Catholic theologies and statements of faith. All this seems in line with the kind of unity that befits the Christian community: A Spirit-led community, a lively community in which variety and difference are alien only to the extent that they set brother against brother, only to the extent that differences dim Christian hope.

What about freedom of conscience? How much of this will be encouraged in the Catholic Church?

This is a relatively uncharted area that Catholics are going to have to explore — the problem of authority in the Church in its relation to the individual conscience. Everyone knows that Vatican II issued a declaration of religious liberty which supports the freedom of individuals in worship and religious commitment. The Council showed great respect for the individual consciences of all men. Then some theologians raised the question, soon after the Council ended, whether a "bill of rights" for individual Catholics shouldn't be issued. At first when I heard about this, I thought it was strange. But now I see great point to it.

From another angle, if the visible Church is supposed to be a sign raised among the nations, can it be such a sign of the commitment to it is not a free one, one that is the opposite of automatic, mechanical and simply conformist? The bishops in the Church have the duty of teaching, and of exhorting the people to the fullest, possible commitment to Christ and his activity among men. But couldn't a person have real reservations about a particular formulation of the faith or law? Would it not be hypocritical to go through the motions of accepting something that seems unacceptable? The more truthful posture might be to investigate, inquire, pray, and try to live the Christian life with the honest reservation, to live as a kind of "fellow traveller"?

A person might thus hope that either he would come to see the truth expressed in the formulated law, or that the law would change.

This is an area that requires careful study of the claims of charity, humility, obedience, freedom, and so on. This way, authority would be persuasive rather than prescriptive. It would appeal to the freedom of the Christian rather than to some fear lurking in the shadows.

Theologians like John McKenzie feel that this persuasive kind of authority is more capable of being a witness to the Gospel than a more dictatorial, monarchical, and simply vertical kind of authority. Such prescriptive authority says little to the contemporary world about the freedom that God has called men to share in.

Collegiality, parish councils, priest senates and all the other mechanisms of shared decision-making can make it possible in human terms to foster a kind of commitment that is truly Christian and apostolic.

Without this kind of "free obedience," it is difficult to see how contemporary man will be tempted to share the Christian hope, and to the extent that he is not so tempted, Christianity will have failed in its apostolic mission to be a sign of hope.

Discussion

1) Do you agree with the way in which the Catholic priest talks about Mass, the sacraments, authority in the Church? Does it seem that he changed his viewpoint from that of his early years just to shed his childhood and family influences? Do you know persons like the priest who have changed their outlook toward the Church?

2) Do you think the priest is very sure of his faith? Doesn't he seem to waver, for example, between freedom of conscience and submission to authority? Do you know other Catholics who say they are still "searching," still trying to understand, still trying to make sense of the demands of faith?

3) Would you like it if this priest came to your parish? Do you think he would be helpful in confession, or would he just confuse you with his ideas? Would you like him to teach your children religion in parochial school or in a CCD course? Would the older people in the parish like the kinds of sermons he might give? Do you think he would be a priest who would try to change everything? Would he probably try to have experimental or "underground" Masses?

4) Describe in your own words what you think is the basic dif-

ference in religious belief between the two writers, the Protestant
and the priest. Do you think most of the Catholics and Protestants
you know see their differences in the same way? If not how do they
see them?

Was the Catholic's explanation of his religion the same sort of
explanation that you would give? In what ways would the account
of your Christian viewpoint be the same as this priest's? In what
ways different?

Thinking About the Future

A Russian Scientist's Proposal

Christian hope takes up every human hope and transforms it. Christian hope calls men toward true humanity. Christian hope looks toward the redemption, the re-creation of every human reality.

But so far this book has largely concentrated on the meaning of Christian hope for the individual caught in a world of change. What does Christian hope mean for the whole world, for all mankind? How does the hoping Christian look to the next quarter-century? What kinds of developments and problems does he see? How will military issues, economic problems, political difficulties, social disturbances be handled? Where will we find the tools to deal with the fantastically complex and sophisticated world that is growing up all around us? Will we use the world, or will the world use us? How does Christian hope look toward the future of mankind?

World Problems: Today and Tomorrow

In June of 1968 the prominent Russian physicist Andrei Sakharov published a lengthy paper on the world's problems and the steps he felt were necessary to solve them. He concentrated especially on the responsibilities and problems of the United States and the U.S.S.R. His analysis ranged over a vast area of human suffering and human need: from Stalinism to overpopulation and famine; from the indispensability of intellectual freedom to the necessity of American-Soviet cooperation. But underlying the whole essay was

a conviction that the problems were not insoluble, that man has it in him to solve these problems and meet the major crises within the lifetime of most people living today.

The following are examples of Sakharov's diagnosis of human problems.

An imperiled civilization: "The division of mankind threatens it with destruction. Civilization is imperiled by: a universal thermonuclear war, catastrophic hunger for most of mankind, stupefaction from the narcotic of 'mass culture' and bureaucratized dogmatism, a spreading of mass myths that put entire peoples and continents under the power of cruel and treacherous demagogues, and destruction or degeneration from the unforeseeable consequences of swift changes in the conditions of life on our planet."

The threat of nuclear war: "The detonation of such a warhead over a city would create a one hundred square kilometer [forty square mile] area of total destruction and fire. Tens of millions of square meters of living space would be destroyed. No fewer than a million people would perish under the ruins of buildings, from fire and radiation, suffocate in the dust and smoke or die in shelters buried under debris. In the event of a ground-level explosion, the fallout of radioactive dust would create a danger of fatal exposure in an area of tens of thousands of square kilometers."

The lack of intellectual freedom: ". . . intellectual freedom is essential to human society . . . Freedom of thought is the only guarantee of the feasibility of a scientific democratic approach to politics, economy, and culture."

New Principles Proposed

Reason and democracy in international affairs: "International affairs must be completely permeated with scientific methodology and a democratic spirit, with a fearless weighing of all facts, views and theories, with maximum publicity of ultimate and intermediate goals and with a consistency of principles.

"The international policies of the world's two leading superpowers (the United States and the Soviet Union) must be based on a universal acceptance of unified and general principles, which we initially would formulate as follows:

"All peoples have the right to decide their own fate with a free expression of their will.

"All military and military-economic forms of export of revolution and counter-revolution are illegal and are tantamount to aggression.

"All countries strive toward mutual help in economic, cultural and general-organizational problems with the aim of eliminating painlessly all domestic and international difficulties and preventing a sharpening of international tensions and a strengthening of the forces of reaction."

Humanitarian spirit: "Specialists are paying attention to a growing threat of hunger in the poorer half of the world. Although 50 per cent increase of the world's population in the last 30 years has been accompanied by a 70 per cent increase in food production, the balance in the poorer half of the world has been unfavorable. The situation in India, Indonesia, in a number of countries of Latin America and in a large number of their undeveloped countries — the absence of technical-economic reserves, competent officials and cultural skills, social backwardness, a high birth rate — all this systematically worsens the food balance and without doubt will continue to worsen it in the coming years.

"The answer would be a wide application of fertilizers, an improvement of irrigation systems, better farm technology, wider use of the resources of the oceans and a gradual perfection of the production, already technically feasible, of synthetic foods, primarily amino acids. However, this is all fine for the rich nations. In the more backward countries, it is apparent from an analysis of the situation and existing trends that an improvement cannot be achieved in the near future, before the expected date of tragedy, 1975–80. . . .

"What is needed most of all is economic and technical assistance to these countries. This assistance must be of such scale and generosity that it is absolutely impossible until the estrangement in the world and the egotistical, narrow-minded approach to relations between nations and races is eliminated.

'The threat of hunger cannot be eliminated without the assistance of the developed countries, and this requires significant changes in their foreign and domestic policies."

The need for U.S. idealism and generosity: "It is necessary to change the psychology of the American citizens so that they will voluntarily and generously support their government and worldwide efforts to change the economy, technology and level of living of bil-

lions of people. This, of course, would entail a serious decline in
the United States rate of economic growth. The Americans should
be willing to do this solely for the sake of lofty and distant goals,
for the sake of preserving civilization and mankind on our planet.

"Similar changes in the psychology of people and practical activities of governments must be achieved in the Soviet Union and
other developed countries."

Other Kinds of Problems

Pollution of Environment: "We live in a swiftly changing world.
Industrial and water-engineering projects, cutting of forests, plowing
up of virgin lands, the use of poisonous chemicals — all this is changing the face of the earth, our 'habitat.'

"Scientific study of all the interrelationships in nature and the
consequences of our interference clearly lag behind the changes.
Large amounts of harmful wastes of industry and transport are being
dumped into the air and water, including cancer-inducing substances.
Will the safe limit be passed everywhere, as has already happened
in a number of places?"

Police dictatorships: "An extreme reflection of the dangers confronting modern social development is the growth of racism, nation-
alism and militarism, and, in particular, the rise of demagogic, hypocritical and monstrously cruel dictatorial police regimes. Foremost
are the regimes of Stalin, Hitler and Mao Tse-Tung, and a number
of extremely reactionary regimes in smaller countries, Spain, Por-
tugal, South Africa, Greece, Albania, Haiti and other Latin-Ameri-
can countries."

The Stalinist period: "Fascism lasted twelve years in Germany.
Stalinism lasted twice as long in the Soviet Union. There are many
common features but also certain differences. Stalinism exhibited a
much more subtle kind of hypocrisy and demagogy, with reliance
not on an openly cannibalistic program like Hitler's, but on a progressive, scientific and popular socialist ideology.

"At least ten to fifteen million people perished in the torture cham-
bers of the N.K.V.D. [secret police] from torture and execution,
in camps for exiled kulaks [rich farmers] and so-called semi-kulaks
and members of their families, and in camps 'without the right of
correspondence' (which were in fact the prototypes of Fascist death
camps where, for example, thousands of prisoners were machine-

gunned because of 'overcrowding' or as a result of 'special orders').

"The inhuman character of Stalinism was demonstrated by the repressions of prisoners of war who survived Fascist camps and then were thrown into Stalinist camps, the antiworker 'decrees,' the criminal exile of entire peoples condemned to slow death, the unenlightened zoological kind of anti-semitism that was characteristic of Stalinist bureaucracy and the N.K.V.D. (and Stalin personally), the Ukrainophobia characteristic of Stalin and the draconian laws for the protection of socialist property (five years' imprisonment for stealing some grain from the fields and so forth) that served mainly as a means of fulfilling the demands of the 'slave market.' "

The threat to intellectual freedom: "This is a threat to the independence and worth of the human personality, a threat to the meaning of human life.

"Nothing threatens freedom of the personality and the meaning of life like war, poverty, terror. But there are also indirect and only slightly more remote dangers.

"One of these is the stupefaction of man (the 'gray mass', to use the cynical term of bourgeois prognosticators) by mass culture with its intentional or commercially motivated lowering of intellectual level and content, with its stress in entertainment or utilitarianism, and with its carefully protective censorship.

"Another example is related to the question of education. A system of education under government control, separation of school and church, universal free education — all these are great achievements of social progress. But everything has a reverse side. In this case it is excessive standardization, extending to the teaching process itself, to the curriculum, especially in literature, history, civics, geography, and to the system of examinations. . . ."

"Modern technology and mass psychology constantly suggest new possibilities of managing the norms of behavior, the strivings and convictions of masses of people. This involves not only management through information based on the theory of advertising and mass psychology, but also more technical methods that are widely discussed in the press abroad.

"Man must not be turned into a chicken or a rat as in the well known experiment in which elation is induced electrically. . . . Related to this is the question of the ever increasing use of tranquilizers. . . .

"Today the key to a progressive restructuring of the system of government in the interests of mankind lies in intellectual freedom."

The Basis for Human Hope

Capitalism and socialism: "The prospects of socialism now depend on whether socialism can be made attractive, whether the moral attractiveness of the ideas of socialism and the glorification of labor, compared with the egotistical ideas of private ownership and the glorification of capital, will be the decisive factors that people will bear in mind when comparing socialism, or whether people will remember mainly the limitations of intellectual freedom under socialism or, even worse, the fascistic regime of the cult [of personality].

"I am placing the accent on the moral aspect because, when it comes to achieving a high productivity of social labor or developing all productive forces or insuring a high standard of living for most of the population, capitalism and socialism seem to have 'played to a tie.' Let us examine this question in detail.

"Imagine two skiers racing through deep snow. At the start of the race, one of them, in striped jacket, was many kilometers ahead, but now the skier in the red jacket is catching up to the leader. What can we say about their relative strength? Not very much, since each skier is racing under different conditions. The striped one broke the snow, and the red one did not have to. (The reader will understand that this ski race symbolizes the burden of research and development costs that the country leading in technology has to bear.) All one can say about the race is that there is not much difference in strength between the two skiers.

"The parable does not, of course, reflect the whole complexity of comparing economic and technological progress in the United States and the Soviet Union, the relative vitality of RRS and AME (Russian Revolutionary Sweep and American Efficiency). . . ."

"1) We have demonstrated the vitality of the socialist course, which has done a great deal for the people materially, cuturally and socially and, like no other system, has glorified the moral significance of labor.

"2) There are no grounds for asserting, as is often done in the dogmatic vein, that the capitalist mode of production leads the economy into a blind alley or that it is obviously inferior to the socialist mode in labor productivity, and there are certainly no grounds for asserting that capitalism always leads to absolute impoverishment of the working class.

"The continuing economic progress being achieved under capitalism would be a fact of great theoretical significance for any nondogmatic Marxist. . . . Both capitalism and socialism are capable of long-term development, borrowing positive elements from each other and actually coming closer to each other in a number of essential aspects."

Two systems compared: "We will now compare the distribution of personal income and consumption for various social groups in the United States and the Soviet Union. . . .

"I have no intention of minimizing the tragic aspects of the poverty, lack of rights and humiliation of the twenty-two million American Negroes. But we must clearly understand that this problem is not primarily a class problem, but a racial problem, involving the racism and egotism of the white workers, and that the ruling group in the United States is interested in solving this problem. . . . It seems to me that we in the socialist camp should be interested in letting the ruling group in the United States settle the Negro problem without aggravating the situation in that country.

"At the other extreme, the presence of millionaires in the United States is not a serious economic burden in view of their small number. The total consumption of the rich is less than 20 per cent, that is, less than the total rise of national consumption over a five-year period. From this point of view, a revolution, which would be likely to halt economic progress for more than five years, does not appear to be an economically advantageous move for the working people. . . .

"Forty per cent of the Soviet population is in difficult economic circumstances. In the United States about 25 per cent of the population is on the verge of poverty. On the other hand the 5 per cent of the Soviet population that belong to the managerial group is as privileged as its counterpart in the United States."

The managerial group: "I want to emphasize that I am not opposed to the socialist principle of payment based on the amount and quality of labor. Relatively higher wages for better administrators, for highly skilled workers, teachers and physicians, for workers in dangerous or harmful occupations, for workers in science, culture and the arts, all of whom account for a relatively small part of the total wage bill, do not threaten society if they are not accompanied by concealed privileges; moreover, higher wages benefit society if they are deserved."

Harmonious relations: "Summing up, we now come to our basic conclusion about the moral and ethical character of the advantages of the socialist course of development of human society. In our view, this does not in any way minimize the significance of socialism. Without socialism, bourgeois practicalism and the egotistical principle of private ownership gave rise to the 'people of the abyss' described by Jack London and earlier by Engels.

"Only the competition with socialism and the pressure of the working class made possible the social progress of the twentieth century and . . . will insure the now inevitable process of rapprochement of the two systems. . . .

"The capitalist world could not help giving birth to the socialist, but now the socialist world should not seek to destroy by force the ground from which it grew. Under the present conditions this would be tantamount to suicide of mankind. Socialism should ennoble that ground by its example and other indirect forms of pressure and then merge with it. . . .

"Such a rapprochement implies not only wide social reforms in the capitalist countries, but also substantial changes in the structure of ownership, with a greater role played by government and cooperative ownership, and the preservation of the basic present features of ownership of the means of production in the socialist countries. . . .

"Bertrand Russell once told a peace congress in Moscow that 'the world will be saved from thermonuclear annihilation if the leaders of each of the two systems prefer complete victory of the other system to a thermonuclear war' (I am quoting from memory). It seems to me that such a solution would be acceptable to the majority of people in any country, whether capitalist or socialist. I consider that the leaders of the capitalist and socialist systems by the very nature of things will gradually be forced to adopt the point of view of the majority of mankind.

"Intellectual freedom of society will facilitate and smooth the way for this trend toward patience, flexibility and a security from dogmatism, fear and adventurism. All mankind, including its best organized and active forces, the working class and the intelligentsia, is interested in freedom and security."

Proposals Summarized

"1) The strategy of peaceful coexistence and collaboration must be deepened in every way. Scientific methods and principles of international policy will have to be worked out, based on scientific prediction of the immediate and more distant consequences.

"2) The initiative must be seized in working out a broad program of struggle against hunger.

"3) A law on the news press and information must be drafted, widely discussed and adopted, with the aim not only of ending irresponsible and irrational censorship, but of encouraging self-study in our society, fearless discussion and the search for truth.

"4) All anticonstitutional laws and decrees violating human rights must be abrogated.

"5) Political prisoners must be amnestied and some of the recent political trials must be reviewed. . . .

"6) The exposure of Stalin must be carried through to the end, to the complete truth, and not just to the carefully weighed half-truth dictated by caste considerations. . . .

"7) The economic reform must be deepened in every way and the area of experimentation expanded, with conclusions based on the results.

"8) A law on geohygiene must be adopted after broad discussion, and ultimately become part of world efforts in this area. . . ."

How Does Christian Hope Respond?

The sweep of Professor Sakharov's vision is awesome. He moves from the threat of nuclear war to the need for intellectual freedom. He moves from international relations to overpopulation, from the American Negro to the pollution of earth. He considers Hitler, Stalin, and Mao as well as the dictatorships of the free world. He summarizes the condition of world affairs and he projects possible paths of peace and prosperity.

In short, Sakharov has tried to spell out the problems which confront mankind as a whole and has labored valiantly to provide meaningful answers. American Christians can only rejoice that so much of what he says seems so reasonable and intelligent in comparison to the dogmatic propagandizing, the shoe-banging, and missile-waving that have marked Russian politics in the second half of the twentieth century. Christians who hope can gladly join in the conversation with him, recognizing common problems and the value of the search for common answers.

In response, Christian hope has certain insights of its own to bring to bear on the problems of the future.

The Soviet physicist seems to put his faith in the "scientific, democratic approach to politics, economics and culture." He sees man's problems being solved by a rational human approach. "International affairs must be completely permeated with scientific methodology and a democratic spirit. . . ." He seems to feel it is only logical for Americans to give up their economic primacy: "They will voluntarily and generously support their government and world-wide efforts to change the economy . . . of millions of people. This would, of course, entail a serious decline in the United States' rate of economic growth. The American should be willing to do this solely for the sake of lofty and distant goals." And so on. Sakharov clearly feels that all human problems are capable of human solutions, and maybe soon.

Furthermore, there is a curious contradiction in Sakharov's writing. While he sees clearly the excesses and horrors of Stalinism — indeed he recounts them at great length — he really cannot account for them. He simply states that Stalinism existed, but he cannot explain it.

A Christian might ask: Did not the horrors and excesses of Stalinism stem from the very approach Sakharov proposes for solving the problems of tomorrow? The Bolsheviks began with high ideals when they took over Russia in 1917 and set about creating a modern industrial state whose profits would be given to the workers. Liberals all over the world were fascinated by the possibilities of the new Soviet state. But within twenty years, Stalin had clamped down with a tyranny unmatched since the days of Genghis Khan.

Is it possible that the Communists' human ideals were in a way the cause of their slide into Stalinism? They saw evil in the world and wanted to overcome it. But when they set out to do so, they failed to see that the policies, the means adopted to achieve their ends, could have disastrous results.

They vastly underrated man's human twistedness and the effects of the use of force to achieve their predetermined ends. In their obsessive pursuit of an immediate earthly paradise, they ended by slaughtering millions and virtually enslaving hundreds of millions.

Sakharov's proposals suffer from the same defect: human fallibility. To take one example: he would have the American economy, across a 15-year period, slow its own growth rate so that the undeveloped world can develop quickly.

The question is not whether American Christians recognize a special responsibility for underdeveloped nations. We do, increasingly. The essential question is: How effective would Sakharov's proposals be? Can any country's economy be built *from the ground up* by outside aid?

The only instance in modern times when this has worked on a large scale was in the years when the Marshall Plan financed the rebuilding of a Europe devastated by World War II. But the Europeans were highly skilled and disciplined people who needed only moderate help to *regain* what they had lost. It is highly questionable that massive aid to underdeveloped countries would work in practice. Indeed, Gunnar Myrdal's classic study of Southeast Asia in *The Asian Dilemma* concludes that the wealthy industrial nations could at best render only marginal aid, such as technical assistance, to the countries of this area.

Why? Nations simply cannot be built from scratch by massive infusions of foreign aid. First, a nation requires an efficient agricultural base. An underdeveloped region must be able to feed itself; otherwise any economic developments it might make would be offset by the need to import food to feed its hungry.

Second, an underdeveloped region needs to develop its agriculture to the point where it has freed a large part of its people from working the land. If its farming is so inefficient that seventy or eighty per cent of the people are required to feed the nation, there cannot be a working force large enough to build industry. By contrast, in the United States less than ten per cent of the people work in farming; this frees the rest of the U.S. working force for industrial, commerical, and service occupations.

Third, the people of an underdeveloped nation need to be reasonably self-disciplined and honest. While Western nations take no special prizes for their honesty, in much of the non-Western world dishonesty is practically a way of life. Economic growth is very difficult without the contracts, credit, and human trust that are so commonplace to us.

Fourth, the underdeveloped nations have to educate their people toward the goals they all seek. Until this is accomplished, even a highly educated minority (as exists in India) will find it difficult to make progress.

Finally, underdeveloped nations need social institutions they often don't have, like reasonably honest local governments and courts of justice.

Thus it is not so easy to "build" advanced nations out of underdeveloped ones, as Sakharov seems to think. Technological and educational assistance is doubtless imperative, but it is doubtful that even massive efforts by the United States and the other industrial nations could remold the underdeveloped world. In fact, this world Sakharov proposes to help might well be injured by an ill-considered attempt. Enormous American economic aid to South Vietnam has resulted in the disruption of the native culture, the breakdown of national morality, and the rise to power of sometimes unprincipled men. If we did the same damage to ten or twenty other nations, the results could be catastrophic.

Besides, the powerhouse of the U.S. economy might be paralyzed by a hurried effort to pour billions into countries which are simply incapable of absorbing them. Nation building is a long and complex process. It is not to be lightly undertaken, as if it could be accomplished in fifteen or twenty years.

Furthermore, a too optimistic effort — based on the assumption that man can more or less instantly remold his world — might lead to generations of class war, to a kind of new colonialism, and consequently to bitter hatred of the United States. Russia already has such a legacy in the states of Eastern Europe because Stalin tried to remold them in his own image. From the East German riots of 1953, through the Hungarian revolt of 1956, to the Czechoslovak liberalization efforts of 1968, the Eastern Europeans have tried to say "No." Sakharov wants to "wash off the blood and dirt that have befouled [the Soviet] banner." But he fails to see that the very effort to seize and transform the world in a single, rational, "scientific" step could lead to exactly the repression and brutality that he rejects.

Nonetheless, the difficulties of humanizing mankind should not cripple us into inactivity. Sakharov's hopefulness is an excellent thing.

The Vision of Vatican II

Vatican II gave its own guidelines for the recreation of a world where men are fallible. It tried to place the humanization of man *and* human fallibility within the framework of the saving work of Christ. In the Pastoral Constitution on *The Church in the Modern World* we find the Council speaking of ". . . the world of men, the whole human family along with the sum of those realities in the midst of which that family lives. It gazes upon that world which is the theater of man's history, and carries the marks of his energies, his tragedies, and his triumphs; that world which the Christian sees as created and sustained by its Maker's love, fallen indeed into the bondage of sin, yet emancipated now by Christ. He was crucified and rose again to break the stranglehold of personified Evil, so that this world might be fashioned anew according to God's design and reach its fulfilment. . . .

"Today, the human race is passing through a new stage of its history. Profound and rapid changes are spreading by degrees around

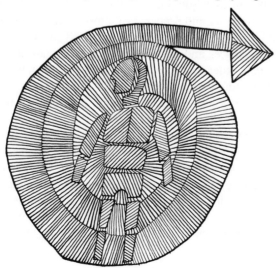

the whole world. Triggered by the intelligence and creative energies of man, these changes recoil upon him, upon his decisions and desires, both individual and collective, and upon his manner of thinking and acting with respect to things and to people. Hence we can already speak of a true social and cultural transformation, one which has repercussions on man's religious life as well. . . .

"As happens in any crisis of growth, this transformation has brought serious difficulties in its wake. Thus while man extends his power in every direction, he does not always succeed in subjecting it to his own welfare. Striving to penetrate farther into the deeper recesses of his own mind, he frequently appears more unsure of himself. Gradually and more precisely he lays bare the laws of society, only to be paralyzed by uncertainty about the direction to give it.

"Never has the human race enjoyed such an abundance of wealth, resources, and economic power. Yet a huge proportion of the world's citizens is still tormented by hunger and poverty, while countless numbers suffer from total illiteracy. Never before today has man been so keenly aware of freedom, yet at the same time, new forms of social and psychological slavery make their appearance."

A Changing World

The Council recognizes that the human race is passing through a period of radical change and development.

"Today's spiritual agitation and the changing conditions of life are part of a broader and deeper revolution. As a result of the latter, intellectual formation is ever increasingly based on the mathematical and natural sciences and on those dealing with man himself, while in the practical order the technology which stems from these sciences takes on mounting importance.

"This scientific spirit exerts a new kind of impact on the cultural sphere and on modes of thought. Technology is now transforming the face of the earth, and is already trying to master outer space. To a certain extent, the human intellect is also broadening its dominion over time: over the past by means of historical knowledge; over the future by the art of projecting and by planning.

"Advances in biology, psychology, and the social sciences not only bring men hope of improved self-knowledge. In conjunction with technical methods, they are also helping men to exert direct influence on the life of social groups. At the same time, the human race is giving ever-increasing thought to forecasting and regulating its own population growth."

These rapid changes call for new and creative responses. The law and custom of our forefathers may no longer suffice.

"Thus, the human race has passed from a rather static concept of reality to a more dynamic, evolutionary one. In consequence, there has arisen a new series of problems, a series as important as can be, calling for new efforts of analysis and synthesis. . . .

"The institutions, laws, and modes of thinking and feeling as handed down from previous generations do not always seem to be well adapted to the contemporary state of affairs. Hence arises an upheaval in the manner and even the norms of behavior."

Men all over the world are no longer willing to remain in the miserable physical or spiritual situations their fathers endured. They are demanding that all things be made new.

"Meanwhile, the conviction grows not only that humanity can and should increasingly consolidate its control over creation, but even more, that it devolves on humanity to establish a political, social, and economic order which will to an ever better extent serve man and help individuals as well as groups to affirm and develop the dignity proper to them.

"As a result very many persons are quite aggressively demanding those benefits of which with vivid awareness they judge themselves to be deprived either through injustice or unequal distribution. Nations on the road to progress, like those recently made independent, desire to participate in the goods of modern civilization not only in the political field but also economically, and to play their part freely on the world scene. Still they continually fall behind while very often their dependence on wealthier nations deepens more rapidly, even in the economic sphere.

"People hounded by hunger call upon those better off. Where they have not yet won it, women claim for themselves an equity with men before the law and in fact. Laborers and farmers seek not only to provide for the necessities of life but to develop the gifts of their personality by their labors, and indeed to take part in regulating economic, social, political, and cultural life. Now, for the first time in human history, all people are convinced that the benefits of culture ought to be and actually can be extended to everyone.

"Still, beneath all these demands lies a deeper and more widespread longing. Persons and societies thirst for a full and free life worthy of man — one in which they can subject to their own welfare all that the modern world can offer them so abundantly. In addition, nations try harder every day to bring about a kind of universal community.

"Since all these things are so, the modern world shows itself at once powerful and weak, capable of the noblest deeds or the foulest. Before it lies the path to freedom or to slavery, to progress or retreat, to brotherhood or hatred. Moreover, man is becoming aware that it is his responsibility to guide aright the forces which he has unleashed and which can enslave him or minister to him. That is why he is putting questions to himself."

All of these changes can be seen as good and positive, part of the transformation and redemption God is bringing about. They are part of the plan and purpose of the Lord who became incarnate and rose again.

"The Church believes that Christ, who died and was raised up for all, can through His Spirit offer man the light and the strength to measure up to his supreme destiny. Nor has any other name under heaven been given to man by which it is fitting for him to be saved. She likewise holds that in her most benign Lord and Master can be found the key, the focal point, and the goal of all human history.

"Hence in the light of Christ, the image of the unseen God, the firstborn of every creature, the Council wishes to speak to all men in order to illuminate the mystery of man and to cooperate in finding the solution to the outstanding problems of our time."

True Humanity

In light of Christ's resurrection, the true end of man has been revealed, the real nature of humanity has been pointed out. And yet Christ has also made most clear the fearful ambiguity in which men live. They are not only good; they also are involved in evil.

"According to the almost unanimous opinion of believers and unbelievers alike, all things on earth should be related to man as their center and crown.

"But what is man? About himself he has expressed, and continues to express, many divergent and even contradictory opinions. In these he often exalts himself as the absolute measure of all things or debases himself to the point of despair. The result is doubt and anxiety.

"For sacred Scripture teaches that man was created 'to the image of God,' is capable of knowing and loving his Creator, and was appointed by Him as master of all earthly creatures that he might subdue them and use them to God's glory. . . .

"But God did not create man as a solitary. For from the beginning "male and female he created them" (Gen. 1:27). Their companionship produces the primary form of interpersonal communion. For by his innermost nature man is a social being, and unless he relates himself to others he can neither live nor develop his potential.

"Examining his heart, man finds that he has inclinations toward evil too, and is engulfed by manifold ills which cannot come from his good Creator. Often refusing to acknowledge God as his beginning, man has disrupted also his proper relationship to his own ultimate goal. At the same time he became out of harmony with himself, with others, and with all created things.

"Therefore man is split within himself. As a result, all of human life, whether individual or collective, shows itself to be a dramatic struggle between good and evil, between light and darkness. Indeed, man finds that by himself he is incapable of battling the assaults of evil successfully, so that everyone feels as though he is bound by chains.

"But the Lord Himself came to free and strengthen man, renewing him inwardly and casting out that prince of this world (cf. Jn. 12:31) who held him in the bondage of sin. For sin has diminished man, blocking his path to fulfillment.

"The call to grandeur and the depths of misery are both a part of human experience. They find their ultimate and simultaneous explanation in the light of God's revelation."

But human life is not a dreary and morbid struggle with evil. God has granted man the dignity of a free creature. Men can learn to love, can learn what it means to live, can become sons of God. The end of salvation which we have in Christ is not something imposed on men: It is the end and purpose of their creation and growth.

"Only in freedom can man direct himself toward goodness. Our contemporaries make much of this freedom and pursue it eagerly; and rightly so, to be sure. Often, however, they foster it perversely as a license for doing whatever pleases them, even if it is evil.

"For its part, authentic freedom is an exceptional sign of the divine image within man. For God has willed that man be left "in the hand of his own counsel" so that he can seek his Creator spontaneously, and come freely to utter and blissful perfection through loyalty to Him. Hence man's dignity demands that he act according to a knowing and free choice. Such a choice is personally motivated and prompted from within. It does not result from blind internal impulse nor from mere external pressure.

"Man achieves such dignity when, emancipating himself from all captivity to passion, he pursues his goal in a spontaneous choice of what is good, and procures for himself, through effective and skillful action, apt means to that end. Since man's freedom has been damaged by sin, only by the help of God's grace can he bring such a relationship with God into full flower."

The value of humanity cannot, must not, be destroyed in senseless wars and mass murder.

"Coming down to practical and particularly urgent consequences, this Council lays stress on reverence for man; everyone must consider his every neighbor without exception as another self, taking into account first of all his life and the means necessary to living it with dignity, so as not to imitate the rich man who had no concern for the poor man Lazarus.

"Furthermore, whatever is opposed to life itself, such as any type of murder, genocide, abortion, euthanasia, or willful self-destruction, whatever violates the integrity of the human person, such as mutilation, torments inflicted on body or mind, attempts to coerce the will itself; whatever insults human dignity, such as subhuman living conditions, arbitrary imprisonment, deportation, slavery, prostitution, the selling of women and children; as well as disgraceful working conditions, where men are treated as mere tools for profit, rather than as free and responsible persons; all these things and others of their like are infamies indeed."

The infinite worth of humanity is not founded on a "rational" and "scientific" analysis of the world, however. It is founded on the Lordship of our God, who created and redeemed us. Our activities and cares and concerns are valuable exactly because this is what we were given to do, "to subdue the earth and the creatures thereof."

"Throughout the course of the centuries, men have labored to better the circumstances of their lives through a monumental amount of individual and collective effort. To believers, this point is settled: considered in itself, such human activity accords with God's will. For man, created to God's image, received a mandate to subject to himself the earth and all that it contains, and to govern the world with justice and holiness; a mandate to relate himself and the totality of things to Him who was to be acknowledged as the Lord and Creator of all. Thus, by the subjection of all things to man, the name of God would be wonderful in all the earth."

And all the activities of mankind will ultimately be caught up in the redemptive work of Christ.

"We do not know the time for the consummation of the earth and of humanity. Nor do we know how all things will be transformed. As deformed by sin, the shape of this world will pass away. But we are taught that God is preparing a new dwelling place and a new earth where justice will abide, and whose blessedness will answer and surpass all the longings for peace which spring up in the human heart."

The economic sphere is no exception. The humanization of man is and must be worked out in terms of money, property, and labor as well as in other areas.

"In the socio-economic realm, the dignity and total vocation of the human person must be honored and advanced along with the welfare of society as a whole. For man is the source, the center, and the purpose of all socio-economic life.

"As in other areas of social life, modern economy is marked by man's increasing domination over nature, by closer and more intense relationships between citizens, groups, and countries and by their mutual dependence, and by more frequent intervention on the part of government. At the same time progress in the methods of production and in the exchange of goods and services has made the economy an apt instrument for meeting the intensified needs of the human family more successfully.

"Reasons for anxiety, however, are not lacking. Many people, especially in economically advanced areas, seem to be hypnotized, as it were, by economics, so that almost their entire personal and social life is permeated with a certain economic outlook. These people can be found both in nations which favor a collective economy as well as in others.

"Again, we are at a moment in history when the development of economic life could diminish social inequalities if that development were guided and coordinated in a reasonable and human way. Yet all to often it serves only to intensify the inequalities. In some places it even results in a decline in the social status of the weak and in contempt for the poor.

"While an enormous mass of people still lack the absolute necessities of life, some, even in less advanced countries, live sumptuously or squander wealth. Luxury and misery rub shoulders. While the few enjoy very great freedom of choice, the many are deprived of almost all possibility of acting on their own initiative and responsibility, and often subsist in living and working conditions unworthy of human beings.

"A similar lack of economic and social balance is to be noted between agriculture, industry, and the services, and also between different parts of one and the same country. The contrast between the economically more advanced countries and other countries is becoming more serious day by day, and the very peace of the world can be jeopardized in consequence."

Economic affairs are not solely the concern of the wealthy and powerful few. They involve all men, so all people should participate in their administration regulation.

"Economic development must be kept under the control of mankind. It must not be left to the sole judgment of a few men or groups possessing excessive economic power, or of the political community alone, or of certain especially powerful nations. It is proper, on the contrary, that at every level the largest possible number of people have an active share in directing that development. When it is a question of international developments, all nations should so participate. It is also necessary for the spontaneous activities of individuals and of independent groups to be coordinated with the efforts of public authorities. These activities and these efforts should be aptly and harmoniously interwoven."

Vast economic inequalities are dehumanizing and must be adjusted. At the same time violence between rich and poor can often tear a society to shreds. It must be avoided if at all possible.

"If the demands of justice and equity are to be satisfied, vigorous efforts must be made, without violence to the rights of persons or to the natural characteristics of each country, to remove as quickly as possible the immense economic inequalities which now exist. In many cases, these are worsening and are connected with individual and group discrimination."

The humanization or dehumanization of man must take precedence over issues of efficiency and capital. The latter are only tools toward the achievement of the former.

"Human labor which is expended in the production and exchange of goods or in the performance of economic services is superior to the other elements of economic life. For the latter have only the nature of tools."

Conditions of work, wages, and personal needs must be taken into account. Human economic life must be structured around human beings, not around abstract economic theories.

"From all these considerations there arise every man's duty to labor faithfully and also his right to work. It is the duty of society, moreover, according to the circumstances prevailing in it, and in keeping with its proper role, to help its citizens find opportunities for adequate employment. Finally, payment for labor must be such as to furnish a man with the means to cultivate his own material, social, cultural, and spiritual life worthily, and that of his dependents. What this payment should be will vary according to each man's assignment and productivity, the conditions of his place of employment, and the common good.

"Since economic activity is generally exercised through the combined labors of human beings, any way of organizing and directing that activity which would be detrimental to any worker would be wrong and inhuman. It too often happens, however, even in our day, that in one way or another workers are made slaves of their work. This situation can by no means be justified by so-called economic laws. The entire process of productive work, therefore, must be adapted to the needs of the person and to the requirements of his life, above all his domestic life. Such is especially the case with respect to mothers of families, but due consideration must be given to every person's sex and age."

Workers must have the right to organize and bargain collectively for their own welfare.

"In economic enterprises it is persons who work together, that is, free and independent human beings created to the image of God. Therefore the active participation of everyone in the running of an enterprise should be promoted. This participation should be exercised in appropriately determined ways. It should take into account each person's function, whether it be one of ownership, hiring, management, or labor. It should provide for the necessary unity of operations.

"However, decisions concerning economic and social conditions, on which the future of the workers and their children depends, are rather often made not within the enterprise itself but by institutions on a higher level. Hence the workers themselves should have a share also in controlling these institutions, either in person or through freely elected delegates.

"The distribution of goods should be directed toward providing employment and sufficient income for the people of today and of the future. Whether individuals, groups, or public authorities make the decisions concerning this distribution and the planning of the economy, they are bound to keep these objectives in mind."

On the other hand, private property is necessary for the exercise of individual interests and provides a bulwark for civil rights.

"Ownership and other forms of private control over material goods contribute to the expression of personality. Moreover, they furnish men with an occasion for exercising their role in society and in the economy. Hence it is very important to facilitate the access of both individuals and communities to some control over material goods.

"Private ownership or some other kind of dominion over material goods provides everyone with a wholly necessary area of independence, and should be regarded as an extension of human freedom. Finally, since it adds incentives for carrying on one's function and duty, it constitutes a kind of prerequisite for civil liberties."

But private property has a social dimension and cannot be divorced from public responsibility.

"By its very nature, private property has a social quality deriving from the law of the communal purpose of earthly goods. If this social quality is overlooked, property often becomes an occasion of greed and of serious disturbances. Thus, to those who attack the concept of private property, a pretext is given for calling the right itself into question."

Christian participation in economic activity can be a significant function in working out the humanity of man.

"Christians who take an active part in modern socio-economic development and defend justice and charity should be convinced that they can make a great contribution to the prosperity of mankind and the peace of the world. Whether they do so as individuals or in association, let their example be a shining one. After acquiring in faithfulness to Christ and His Gospel observe the right order of values in their earthly activities."

Rights of Men

An aspect of the humanization of man is his right to participate freely and without fear in his government.

"Our times have witnessed profound changes too in the institutions of peoples and in the ways that peoples are joined together. These changes are resulting from the cultural, economic, and social evolution of these same peoples. The changes are having a great impact on the life of the political community, especially with regard to universal rights and duties both in the exercise of civil liberty and in the attainment of the common good, and with regard to the regulation of the relations of citizens among themselves, and with public authority.

"From a keener awareness of human dignity there arises in many parts of the world a desire to establish a political-juridical order in which personal rights can gain better protection. These include the rights of free assembly, of common action, of expressing personal opinions, and of professing a religion both privately and publicly. For the protection of personal rights is a necessary condition for the active participation of citizens, whether as individuals or collectively, in the life and government of the state."

Justice is an essential bulwark of *human* society.

"Men are voicing disapproval of any kind of government which blocks civil or religious liberty, multiplies the victims of ambition and political crimes, and wrenches the exercise of authority from pursuing the common good to serving the advantage of a certain faction or of the rulers themselves. There are some such governments holding power in the world.

"No better way exists for attaining a truly human political life then by fostering an inner sense of justice, benevolence, and service for the common good, and by strengthening basic beliefs about the true nature for the political community, and about the proper exercise and limits of public authority."

Indeed, the people's participation in their government is essential to the fulfillment of human nature.

"It is in full accord with human nature that juridical-political structures should, with ever better success and without any discrimination, afford all their citizens the chance to participate freely and actively in establishing the constitutional bases of a political community, governing the state, determining the scope and purpose of various institutions, and choosing leaders."

Peace

Unless world peace is established the humanization of man cannot go on.

In our generation when men continue to be afflicted by acute hardships and anxieties arising from ongoing wars or the threat of them, the whole human family has reached an hour or supreme crisis in its advance toward maturity. Moving gradually together and everywhere more conscious already of its oneness, this family cannot accomplish its task of constructing for all men everywhere a world more genuinely human unless each person devotes himself with renewed determination to the reality of peace.

"Peace is not merely the absence of fear. Nor can it be reduced solely to the maintenance of a balance of power between enemies. Nor is it brought about by dictatorship. Instead, it is rightly and appropriately called "an enterprise of justice" (Is. 32:7). Peace results from that harmony built into human society by its divine Founder, and actualized by men as they thirst after ever greater justice."

The fierceness of new weapons and the horrors of protracted guerilla warfare make peace imperative.

"In spite of the fact that recent wars have wrought physical and moral havoc on our world, conflicts still produce their devasting effect day by day somewhere in the world. Indeed, now that every kind of weapon produced by modern science is used in war, the fierce character of warfare threatens to lead the combatants to a savagery far surpassing that of the past. Furthermore, the complexity of the modern world and the intricacy of international relations allow guerilla warfare to be drawn out by new methods of deceit and subversion. In many cases the use of terrorism is regarded as a new way to wage war.

"The horror and peversity of war are immensely magnified by the multiplication of scientific weapons. For acts of war involving these weapons can inflict massive and indiscriminate destruction far exceeding the bounds of legitimate defense. Indeed, if the kind of instruments which can now be found in the armories of the great nations were to be employed to their fullest, an almost total and altogether reciprocal slaughter of each side by the other would follow, not to mention the widespread devastation which would take place in the world and the deadly aftereffects which would be spawned by the use of such weapons."

Thus it is absolutely necessary to work toward ultimate peace and to work for every possible alleviation of hostility.

"It is our clear duty, then, to strain every muscle as we work for the time when all war can be completely outlawed by international consent. This goal undoubtedly requires the establishment of some universal public authority acknowledged as such by all, and endowed with effective power to safeguard, on the behalf of all, security, regard for justice, and respect for rights.

"But before this hoped-for authority can be set up, the highest existing international centers must devote themselves vigorously to the pursuit of better means for obtaining common security. Peace must be born of mutual trust between nations, rather than imposed on them through fear of one another's weapons. Hence everyone must labor to put an end at last to the arms race, and to make a true beginning of disarmament, not indeed a unilateral disarmament, but one proceeding at an equal pace according to agreement, and backed up by authentic and workable safeguards."

Aid to Underdeveloped Nations

The advanced nations in the world must make every effort to help the underdeveloped world, while refusing to engage in ideological struggles.

"The developing nations will be unable to procure the necessary material assistance unless the practices of the modern business world undergo a profound change. Additional help should be offered by advanced nations, in the form of either grants or investments. These offers should be made generously and without avarice. They should be accepted honorably.

"If an economic order is to be created which is genuine and universal, there must be an abolition of excessive desire for profit, nationalistic pretensions, the lust for political domination, militaristic thinking, and intrigues designed to spread and impose ideologies.

"In many instances there exists a pressing need to reform economic and social structures. But nations must beware of technical solutions immaturely proposed, especially those which offer men material advantages while militating against his spiritual nature and development. For, "Not by bread alone does man live, but by every word that comes forth from the mouth of God" (Mt. 4:4). Each branch of the human family possesses in itself and in its worthier traditions some part of the spiritual treasure entrusted by God to humanity, even though many do not know the source of this treasure.

"Not everyone who cries, 'Lord, Lord,' will enter into the kingdom of heaven, but those who do the Father's will and take a strong grip on the work at hand. Now, the Father wills that in all men we recognize Christ our brother and love Him effectively in word and in deed. By thus giving witness to the truth, we will share with others the mystery of the heavenly Father's love. As a consequence, men throughout the world will be aroused to a lively hope — the gift of the Holy Spirit — that they will finally be caught up in peace and utter happiness in that fatherland radiant with the splendor of the Lord."

Thus Vatican II provides Christian hope with a context for the continuing humanization of man — without an unleashing of demonic forces that still beset sinful mankind.

We can look toward social, economic, and political progress without leaving the imprint of our inhumanity on it.

We can face the problems that Sakharov outlines — but avoid any dangerous assumption of our omnipotence. We can have faith in the future toward which God draws us, in the new humanity he will recreate in us, in the full manhood he is preparing for us.

Discussion

1) Do you agree with Sakharov's assessment of world problems? Can you agree with his solutions? Do his solutions really avoid the kinds of oppression which the Russian people experienced under Stalin's regime? Discuss any inadequacies you see in his approach. Does Sakharov see the future in the same way you do? Can you understand the motivation from which Sakharov wrote his essay?

2) Are the statements from Vatican II about problems that face mankind more realistic than Sakharov's essay? In discussing solutions to world problems, such as thermonuclear war, world poverty and racial injustice, do Vatican II's recommendations seem to avoid really coming to grips with the problems? Do you agree with the unhasty, careful and tactful approach that Vatican II advises in response to urgent and demanding problems? Do you think that the Church has a responsibility to speak out on matters that are really problems of society and world politics? Or do you think that the Church should not only speak out on these matters, but also should act strongly, vigorously, and immediately? If you think the Church should act, what kind of actions should it take? Does the Church really offer mankind hope in the solution of human problems?

3) Do you feel that this appendix in general is overly idealistic? Do you find yourself asking what practical good it is to make sweeping general statements about world hunger and thermonuclear war when no one can do anything about them? Or is there something an individual can do in these areas? What is the effect of such techniques as picketing and protest marches, sit-ins and boycotts, or writing letters to public newspapers and political leaders? Are there any techniques which have proved effective? Are organized groups more effective in getting themselves heard than individuals? Do you think that people have really explored the possibilities of getting their voices heard?

4) Aren't all the quotations the appendix employs extremely

idealistic? More like wild dreams than practical plans? Is there any kind of national or world government that could carry out such a program? At the same time that world famous men accuse nations of being unconcerned and complacent about problems like world hunger and racial prejudice, couldn't national leaders accuse individual citizens of being unconcerned and complacent? Do you know of individuals or groups in your community that are anything but unconcerned and complacent about these problems? How can anyone accuse the United States government of being unconcerned and complacent in the light of all the aid it has given to underprivileged nations?

Index

241